Celebrating
DIVERSITY
Extended Thematic Unit
by Susan Kane, David Cavanaugh, and Jane Gilbert

Teacher Created Materials

Teacher Created Materials, Inc.

P.O. Box 1040

Huntington Beach, CA 92647

©1993 Teacher Created Materials, Inc.

Made in U.S.A.

ISBN 1-55734-601-1

Edited by
Ina Massler Levin

Illustrated by
Sue Fullam
Keith Vasconcelles
Theresa M. Wright

305.8
c.1

CL
B1

Table of Contents

Introduction

We live in a world rich in diversity. We are people who look different, live in different types of houses, eat different types of food, appreciate different types of arts, wear different types of clothes, and behave in different ways. Yet with our differences, we are in many ways very much the same. We all want to feel a sense of belonging, of caring, and to be valued for being ourselves.

Celebrating Diversity recognizes these feelings. Its unique extended theme format can be used throughout the school year. The units may be rearranged if a different order suits your needs. Each of the units of celebration can in themselves become a school month of study, rich in activities, hands-on experiences, and the building of self-esteem.

The lessons in this book will provide both students and teachers alike an opportunity to share and relish their unique diversity. Through the use of this book students will begin to value their own uniqueness as citizens of the world. They will begin to develop an understanding of the rich diversity of cultures around the world and their contributions to the richness of our lives.

Using an Extended Thematic Unit

What Is Thematic Teaching?

Thematic teaching is a teaching method that allows the teacher to establish an overall interesting idea or a sequence of interesting ideas to which all of the skills and concepts required by the curriculum can be related. Learning experiences need to relate to each other, relate to the needs and experiences of the child, and provide some perspective of the world outside the classroom. Thematic teaching allows for this.

The first step in thematic teaching is choosing a theme. This theme will be your focus in developing a unit for study to incorporate all subject areas for a given length of time. Your theme should easily incorporate several curricular areas.

A central theme should have a broad area of focus. It should be adaptable to as many areas of study, concepts, and skills as possible. A good theme will not only allow flexibility in planning, but also help your students generate connections between subject areas. Bulletin boards and hands-on experiences related to the theme set the atmosphere for the classroom. Writing, research, cooperative-learning projects, and community involvement may all be a part of thematic learning.

Why an Extended Thematic Unit?

Themes can be as short as one day in length or last an entire school year. Although the duration of a theme is an individual choice, *Celebrating Diversity* has been designed to take you through an entire school year. How you use the extended theme in this book will depend greatly on your comfort level with thematic teaching.

Also provided are sub-themes that connect with the central theme of *Celebrating Diversity*. They allow for flexibility. Except for "Celebrating Values," any of the themes may be exchanged for another, so you may use them in the order that is appropriate for you and your individual school calendar.

Celebrating Diversity allows for in-depth study. Since the theme is carried on throughout the year, children are given an opportunity to become immersed in the topic. Activities of wide variety are presented for you to meet your students needs. In addition, a bibliography is provided that will allow you to choose the literature that will enrich your program. The culminating activities are designed to either be done individually or combined as one celebration.

Celebrating Diversity gives you an opportunity to be involved with a theme that, through the year, will allow all the learning that takes place to interconnect, to relate to the needs and experiences of the child, and to provide some perspective of the world outside the classroom.

Celebrating Values, Trust, and Personal Awareness

Begin the introduction of the extended theme by celebrating values, trust, and, personal awareness. Give children the opportunity to explore more about who they are and which values are important in their lives. Explain that trust is an important aspect of getting along, and essential to making the school year a pleasant one. Let each child celebrate that he or she is a unique individual, with feelings that should be respected and valued.

Set up this unit by erecting a bulletin board. A bulletin board that incorporates the children makes them immediately feel a part of the learning. Suggestions for bulletin boards are given on page 6.

You might wish to read some books that let children hear about diversity in people. See the bibliography on pages 143 and 144 for some titles.

Work with students to complete the activities in this section. Each lesson that you teach contains a goal. Choose those that are appropriate for your students. They do not have to be completed in any specific order.

Some of the activities such as the "Coat of Arms" and the calendar, lend themselves to be displayed and will involve the children. Use the calendar activity on pages 19 and 20 and the clip art that follows on page 21. Give each child a calendar and the clip art pages to color. Then let each decide what he or she wishes to celebrate that day.

Make sure that students get to know each other. Complete the "Getting to Know You" interviews. If you opt to videotape them, it will be easy to spread them out over a day or a week.

Build trust and personal awareness with the "Bean Bag Balance" and "Car and Driver."

Regardless of which lessons you choose to undertake with your class, remember to celebrate the children and their learning. This can be as simple as praising them for a job well done or as elaborate as planning a class party. Awards and incentives appropriate for your students can be found on pages 140 and 141.

Mini Table of Contents

Bulletin Board Ideas

Silhouettes

Cover a bulletin board with construction paper, burlap, or wallpaper. Then trace the silhouette of a child's head onto the construction paper. Do this using a light source such as a slide projector. Have each child sit in front of a projector, and then trace his or her profile onto the construction paper. Cut a group of silhouettes in a rainbow of colors. Arrange on the bulletin board, overlapping in an arc. Decide on a title for the bulletin board. Possible titles might include "Good Times Come In Different Colors" or "This Is America."

Full-House Graph

Use a bulletin board to create a Full-House Graph. On a large strip of paper write the question, "How Many Are In My Family?" Under the question place a graph. This can easily be created on a bulletin board using yarn to make rows. Label the rows 1, 2, 3, through 10 or more. Give each child a square of paper or a sticky note on which to write his or her name. Or, if you wish to keep the rows for each number the same color, have several squares of the same color and have children tell you the number of family members before giving them their paper. For each day of the first week the bulletin board is up, have a few children place the squares with the family name in the correct row.

Extension:

Tally the numbers in each group. What does the graph reveal about the number of people in someone's family? Which group has the largest, and which group has the smallest? Challenge the children to tell you what things they have learned from the graph.

Getting To Know You

Goal: To provide an opportunity for students to get to know each other.

Materials: Paper, pencils, interview questions on page 8, (optional: video camera)

Directions: Pair students with a partner they do not know well. Give each student an interview sheet. Review the questions with the students. Have each take a turn asking or interviewing his/her partner for approximately 10-15 minutes. Each should record his/her partner's responses to questions on the interview sheet.

Extensions: Rather than sharing each set of interviews with the class, videotape each set of partners. (A parent volunteer would be helpful for this task.) Show the video at different times during the week. This would also work well as an opening activity; show a few of the interviews at the start of each day.

Interview Questions

Ask your partner these questions. Write down the answer.

What is your name? _____

When is your birthday? _____

How old are you? _____

Where were you born? _____

How many brothers do you have? _____

How many sisters do you have? _____

Do you have a pet? _____

Can you tell me about your pet? _____

_____

What do you like to play? _____

_____

What do you hope to be when you grow up? _____

What is the funniest thing that has ever happened to you? _____

_____

_____

What is the scariest thing that has ever happened to you? _____

_____

_____

Add some questions of your own on the back of this paper.

Bean Bag Balance

Goal: To learn how to take risks.

Materials: One bean bag per child

Direction: Every child puts a bean bag on his or her head, and, on a signal, moves around the room or gym. If the bean bag falls off, the child is frozen. Another child has to risk "losing" his or her bean bag to place the bean bag back on the other child's head. Once the bean bag is replaced, the child is unfrozen and can move around again.

Stop the game after about eight minutes and ask who won. Discuss this with the children. The winners are not the children who kept a bean bag on their head the longest, but any child who helped at least one other child replace his or her bean bag.

Extensions: Make the bean bags. Cut a 5" (13cm) square from tag board to use as a pattern. Using the patterns, cut out two pieces of fabric. Sew them together, leaving a one-inch (2.5 cm) opening on one end. Turn the bean bag inside out. Using large dried beans (such as lima beans), stuff the bag. Sew the one-inch (2.5 cm) opening shut. An alternative to sewing is to use fabric glue. Do not turn the fabric inside out and do not overstuff the bean bags if you glue them. Let the glue dry thoroughly before stuffing and again after shutting the opening.

The Value of Friendship

Goal: To discover what makes a good friend.

Materials: *Rosie and Michael* by Judith Viorst (Atheneum, 1979)

Directions: Read the story *Rosie and Michael.* This is a story about how friendship overcomes all problems. It also portrays a female in a strong, positive role. With the children, brainstorm what makes a good friendship.

On the board, chart paper, or overhead projector draw a chart with two columns. Label one side "Problems or Dilemma" and the other side "Dealing With Problems." Let children help fill in the chart.

Extensions: Have children draw pictures of their best friends.

Problem or Dilemma	Dealing with Problems
Rosie is grouchy.	Michael makes her laugh.
Michael worries a lot.	Rosie understands and shares her fears.
Rosie has freckles.	Michael likes her freckles.
Michael's toes point in, his shoulders droop, and he has hair coming out of his ears.	Rosie likes Michael.
Michael's bird dies.	Rosie comforts him because she's lost a pet, too.
Rosie has a fear of climbing trees.	Michael doesn't have a fear and shows her how.
Michael feels he's a horrible singer.	Rosie loves his voice.

Car and Driver

Goal: To develop trust in each other; to develop concern and compassion for each other; to work for the good of the group.

Materials: None

Directions: Children choose a partner. One partner starts as the driver; the other child starts as the car. The "car" puts his/her hands in front of him/her. These are the bumpers. The car closes his/her eyes. The driver is now responsible for his/her car, and no collisions are allowed. The driver places his/her hands on the car steering wheel (shoulders). The driver backs the car out of the driveway. Have the students use their imagination to take right and left turns, maneuver around the spaces, go on ramps, over bridges, on and off the freeway, stop for red lights, etc. This should continue for about five minutes. Then stop and ask the children how many kept their eyes shut the entire time. Ask the children how they felt when they changed places. Partners should switch, so each gets the experience of being both car and driver.

Coat of Arms

Goal: To discover and express some of the qualities which make each student a unique individual.

Materials: Oak tag or construction paper, crayons, markers, coat of arms pattern (page 13)

Directions: Talk about how students see themselves. Discuss the areas listed below with them. Explain that a coat of arms is a picture on a shield that represents a family. Children may either create a shield of their own or use the pattern on page 13, and make a coat of arms for themselves. Students should include six of the following areas in their design:

What I am best at

What I most need to improve

Hobbies

Family

My past

My future

An animal or bird to represent my family

A color

An important food

Extensions: Let students create a motto or slogan to represent themselves and put it on the ribbon which runs across bottom of the coat of arms.

Coat of Arms Pattern

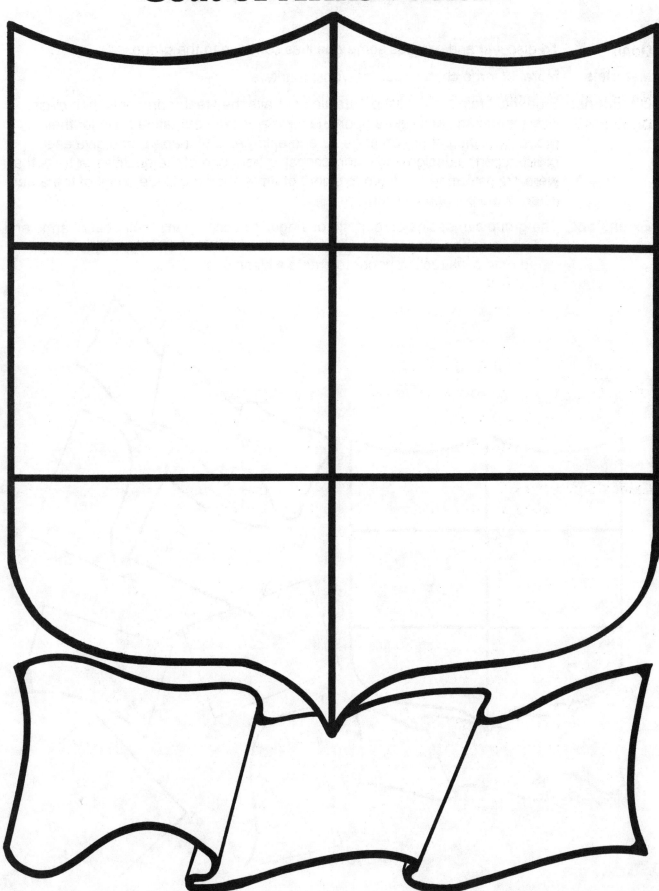

Class Coat of Arms

Goal: To discover and express some qualities common to the group.

Materials: Mural or large chart paper, crayons, markers

Directions: Students brainstorm a list of qualities or traits they feel represents their class. Have them rank and agree upon the six major representative traits for their group. Use the pattern on page 13 and enlarge. Cut it apart, and give each group a part to design and color, choosing from one of the qualities or traits that were brainstormed. The group's coat of arms should include some of the areas listed in the previous lesson.

Extension: The group can decide on a motto or slogan to accompany their coat of arms and write it on ribbon shapes of paper hung below the Coat of Arms. This can be glued onto construction paper to create a class poster.

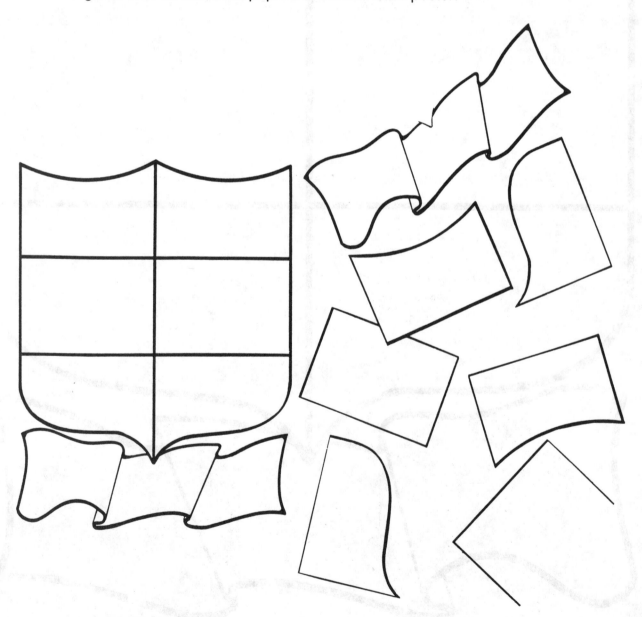

Decision-Making

Goal: To better understand the role of our values in decision-making.

Materials: Copy of the story on page 16.

Directions: Give each student a copy of "John and Henry" or read it to them. After each student reads or hears the story, form small groups and have students talk about the questions below. After answering the questions see if they can determine the values that helped them answer the questions.

Questions for "John and Henry"

1. What would you do if you were Henry?

2. How will John feel when he discovers his bike?

3. What should John tell his Uncle Jack?

4. How do you think Henry felt?

5. What do you think happens next?

6. If you were Henry would you tell someone?

Extensions: Have the children role play. Set up a scene where John finds his bicycle while Henry is with him. Let several pairs act out the parts of John and Henry as John discovers the bicycle with the scratches on it.

John and Henry

John and Henry lived next door to each other. John and Henry were best friends. They always played together after school. Every day they would ride bikes in their neighborhood. John had a beautiful, new, shiny red bike that his Uncle Jack had given to him. "Ride carefully and don't scratch it," said Uncle Jack. "I will," promised John. Henry was jealous of John's new bike. His bike was old and blue, given to him by his brothers after they outgrew it.

One day while John's family was out of town on vacation, Henry decided to ride John's bike. "I'll put it right back and no one will know," thought Henry. "Nothing will happen." Just as he was coming out of John's driveway, Mrs. Olsen's cat darted out in front of Henry. Applying his brakes, Henry realized that he couldn't stop in time. So, he jumped off and the bike went down the hill. It crossed the street, hit the curb, and skidded to a stop. Henry, dazed, picked up the bike and noticed a scratch on the fender. Quickly he raced back to the garage and returned John's bike to the spot where he found it. Henry closed the garage door and headed home.

Role-Playing

Goal: To see how people make decisions.

Materials: *The Lorax* by Dr. Seuss (Random House, 1971); *The Stranger* by Chris Van Allsburg (Houghton Mifflin, 1986); *The Wall* (Clarion, 1992) and *Fly Away Home* (Clarion, 1991) by Eve Bunting

Directions: Read one of the stories aloud. When you have finished discuss the following questions:

1. Do the characters change? If so, how?

2. What problems (conflicts) can you find?

3. Are they resolved well?

4. What questions are you left with?

5. How would you have solved the problem?

The students then role play the story and resolve the conflict to their liking. Their interpretation is not the goal; it's the process that is important.

My Family Heritage—Who Am I?

Goal: To encourage creativity while researching family history.

Materials: Photographs of students, magazines, newspapers, photographs or reproductions of pictures of famous personalities, glue, scissors

Directions: Have children bring in photographs of themselves. Go through old magazines, newspapers, or photographs of famous people. Cut them out. Let children choose a picture of a famous person they can most closely identify with (perhaps the Mona Lisa or a famous sports personality.) Have them glue their photograph onto the face of the famous personality. Label the picture with their name.

Extensions: Let children write a description of themselves. Younger students may need help to do this. Seasons, events, or animals may be substituted for personalities.

Celebration Calendar

Goal: To make a calendar that centers around issues of trust, values, togetherness, and celebration.

Materials: Markers, paint, crayons, pencils, drawing paper, calendar blank (page 20), clip art (page 21), tape or glue

Directions: Begin with a class discussion of the topics of values, trust, personal awareness, and celebrations. Emphasize that the calendars children are about to design, will help to celebrate their diversity. Students then choose to work around a specific topic to decorate their calendars. Give each student a calendar blank and an 11" x 17" (28cm x 43cm) piece of construction paper. Children glue the calendar blank to the construction paper and decorate it. Provide some of the clip art on page 21 for the children to use on the calendar throughout the month as they determine what they feel should be celebrated regarding trust, values, or togetherness. They may also draw pictures or symbols in the calendar boxes.

Extensions: Use the calendars as posters in the classroom, making them accessible to the children to mark or glue on clip art daily to indicate what they wish to share with classmates.

September
(month)

Sunday	Monday	Tuesday	Wednesday	Thursday	Friday	Saturday
		☆			(crayon)	
(bee)						
				(shell)		
		☆ I LIKE YOU!				
		(flag)			☺	

School Calendar

(month)

Sunday	Monday	Tuesday	Wednesday	Thursday	Friday	Saturday

Celebration Calendar (cont.)

Clip Art

   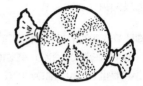

 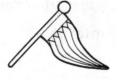 

Celebrating International Arts

Before Celebrating International Arts, review the thematic unit on Celebrating Values, Trust, and Personal Awareness. Spend some time letting children talk about what is important to them. Remind them that what they value may not be as important to others as it is to them. However since they would want people to be respectful of their values, they also should be respectful of others.

As you begin this unit on international arts, help to make children aware that cultures have various types of expression. It takes many different forms. Help them to see the richness in the diversity, by showing the differences in the various activities in which they are about to participate.

Begin by introducing the theme with an "Animals in Arts" bulletin board (page 23). Create a background and let children add animals to it. Ask them questions about it. Find as many different perspectives of the same animals as possible, so children see that although the animals are alike, they can be viewed differently.

As children complete the activities that are included in this section, discuss the cultures from which they come. Talk about the materials that are used, and the fact that often what is available dictates the form the art takes. Let children complete the activities and extend them by interpreting them in their own style.

Add a world map to your classroom (page 142). Highlight the areas of the world from which the art projects originate.

Find pictures of various art forms around the world. Use resource books or magazines. Share these with the children. Let children realize that art is not limited to a painted picture, it can include decoration and ornamentation, as well as useful goods, such as rugs or bowls.

Create an International Art Gallery. Display children's art. Utilize all available bulletin boards. Use covered boxes as stands for jewelry, Egyptian gold, or masks. Cover the walls with sand painting, looms, and fish prints. Invite guests and have the children serve as tour guides. Let your artists celebrate their experiences in the diversity that art allows.

Mini Table of Contents

Bulletin Board Ideas

Animals in Art

Cover the bulletin board with brightly colored paper. Frame it as if it was a picture. This can be accomplished by adding a border made out of color-contrasting, construction paper. Title the bulletin board "Animals in Art."

Find pictures of your favorite animals. Use old magazines or photocopies of pictures for animals. Display some on the bulletin board. Write the discussion questions on the bulletin board. Put them all up at once, or write them on strips and change them. Questions to ask include:

- Name the animals you recognize.
- Would you be afraid to walk among these animals? Why or why not?
- Find profiles and frontal views.
- Which animals seem the most important to you?
- Do the animals look happy, upset, angry? What expressions do they have?
- Are the animals working or playing?
- Do you think these animals belong here?
- Do you think these animals are in danger?

Provide children with paints, paint brushes, and paper. Have them choose one animal that is on the bulletin board and create paintings of that animal to display. Show the children that although the animals are the same, they all look different. Art allows for the differences.

Egyptian Gold

Goal: To experience an ancient Egyptian art form.

Materials: Cardboard or oak tag 6" x 18" (15 cm x 46 cm) or any desired size, aluminum foil, pencil, glue (white liquid in nozzle bottle), handouts of Egyptian symbols and shapes (page 25), yellow permanent marker

Directions: Discuss Egyptian shapes and art forms. Have children choose an interesting Egyptian design from the handouts and glue it to oak tag. Then trace the design with white glue, being careful not to smear it. Let the glue dry thoroughly. This will create a raised outline of the design. Cover with a sheet of aluminum foil. Smooth the foil gently around the design, avoiding the raised areas. Coat the foil with yellow permanent marker. This will produce a relief.

Let children pretend to be archaeologists who have just made a major discovery—Egyptian Gold. A fun way to introduce this is to "hide" a few of the pieces of Egyptian Gold around the room for students to discover. Have them answer the questions on page 26, and write a journal entry on page 27.

Extensions: This works well as a cooperative-team or a total class project designing a mural using poster board. Make sure children complete this on the floor, and then hang it on the wall when finished. The journal entries can be turned into a class book.

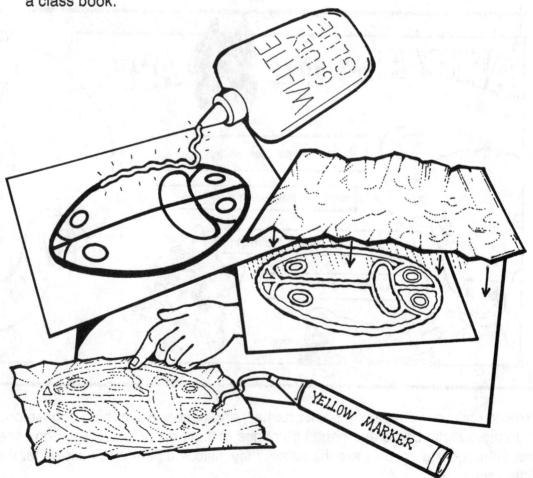

Egyptian Art

You Are an Archaeologist

You have just found Egyptian gold! Soon many people from television and radio will ask you questions. Prepare answers to these questions so you will be ready.

1. Where did you discover your Egyptian gold? _____

_____

2. What were you doing at the time? _____

_____

3. What does it look like? _____

_____

4. What do you think it was used for? _____

_____

5. How did it get to be where you found it? _____

_____

6. What do you think is the value of the Egyptian gold? _____

_____

Journal Entry

Date: _____

Day: _____

Weather: _____

Time: _____

Location: _____

While searching the deserts of Egypt I found _____

_____

_____

_____

_____

_____

_____

Archaeologist

Mask-Making

Goal: To understand the purpose of masks and their significance in different cultures (Eskimo, African, Chinese, Asian, French, American Indian)

Directions: Obtain pictures of masks and people wearing masks from newspapers and magazines. Collect different types of masks. Some possibilities include a bandanna for covering the face, store-bought masks, gas masks, skiers' masks, or surgical masks. Make some sample masks from paper bags, paper, or aluminum plates. (The book, *Masks and Mask Makers,* by Sari Hunt and Bernice Wells Carlson, (Abbington Press, 1961) will serve as a guide on mask-making.)

Activities: Introduce some new vocabulary to children. Include the words masquerade, disguise, festival, ceremony, decorate, decoration, papier-mâché.

Ask children when they wear masks and why? Have they ever seen a picture of anyone wearing a mask? What did it look like? Why was the person wearing it? Why do people all over the world wear masks?

Your discussion can bring out that there are many different kinds of masks all worn for many different reasons. You can explain and discuss gas masks, astronauts' and fire fighters' masks, warm masks for protection against the elements, bandits' masks, masks to transform and disguise the wearer as used in religious ceremonies, fun masks as used in Mardi Gras and at Halloween, and masks in plays.

For homework, have the children do some research. Have them accompany their parents to a store and make a list of the different masks they find. Have them cut up old magazines with pictures of masks or people wearing masks. Let them bring in books from the library about masks. Encourage them to share the information.

A Mask with a Tale

Look at this mask. What does this mask symbolize to you? Describe a celebration or event during which you might wear this mask.

Making Masks

Goal: To give children the opportunity to create their own masks.

Materials: Paper bag, paper or aluminum plates, paint, scissors, glue or tape, bits of foil, yarn or other decorative materials, hole punch, pencil

Directions: Have each child choose the kind of mask they would like to make, such as a Native American or African, or one that he/she feels represents him/her. Masks may be made out of paper bags, or paper or aluminum plates. Decorations might include wool, shells, yarn, or feathers. Have children draw on the mask or cut out and glue or tape the decorations onto it. If children are going to wear the masks, help them determine where the eye holes will go. To wear the masks have them poke a hole using a hole punch or pencil and tie yarn around their heads.

Mask Pattern

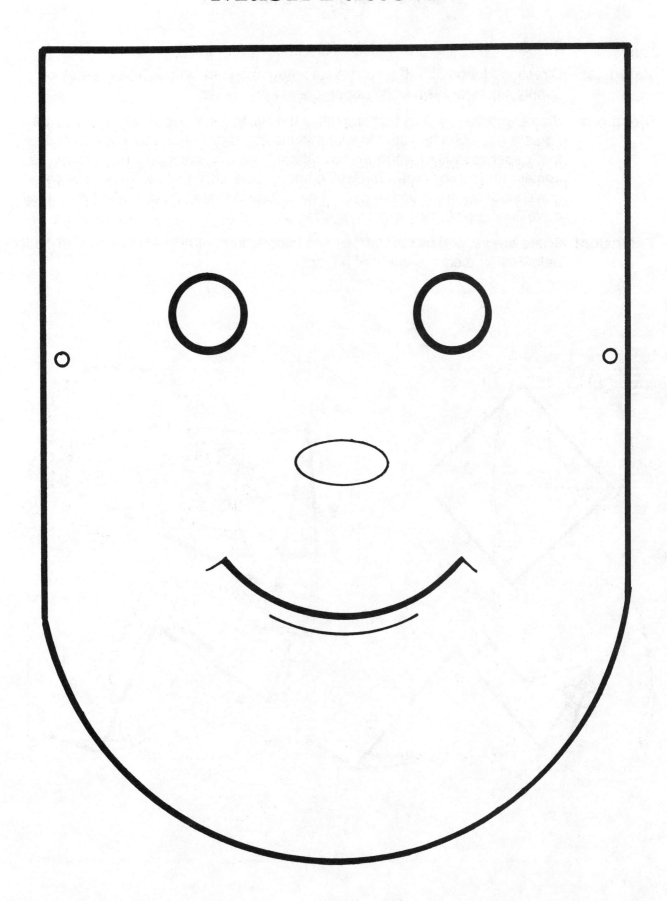

Origami

Goal: To introduce the students to the Japanese art of paper folding.

Materials: Directions (page 33), 6" x 18" (15cm x 45cm) origami paper (available at art supply stores)or plain white paper, crayon or marker

Directions: Share with the children that origami is the Asian art of paper folding. In ancient times it was done by both the wealthy and the poor. At one time it was believed that paper contained spirits and could not be cut. Have students practice this ancient art form by creating a wolf's head. Give each child a piece of paper. Have students listen and follow the directions that are on page 33. When they have finished let them add a wolf's face.

Extension: There are several origami patterns to choose from. Try the simple grasshopper below using a square sheet of paper.

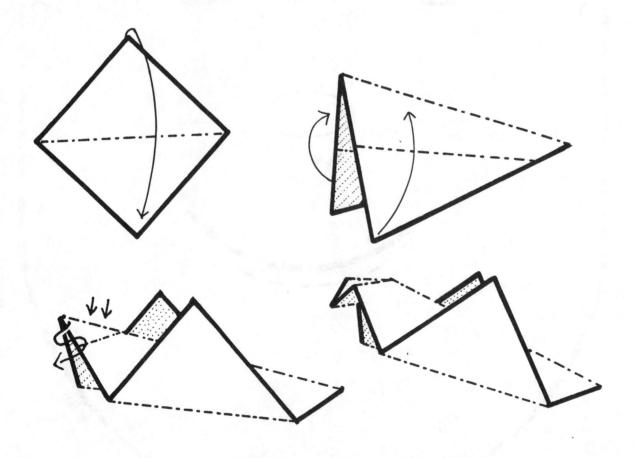

Asian Origami Wolf

Follow these directions to make an origami wolf. Use a piece of brown or gray 6" x 18" (15 cm x 46 cm) construction paper.

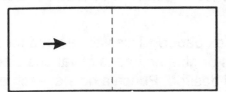

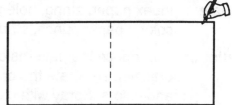

1. Fold the paper in half; bring left edge of paper to right edge. Crease and open.

2. At the top right edge of the paper (about 1" (2.5 cm) from the right corner) make a small dot with a pencil.

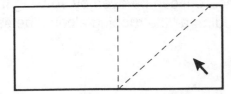

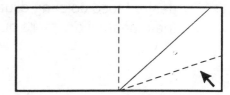

3. Bring lower right corner up to meet the bottom of the center line and the dot. Crease and open the paper.

4. Turn the lower right corner up until it meets the slanted lines.

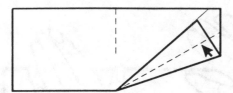

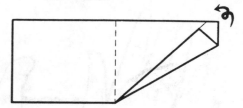

5. Fold this new flap in half, bringing the lower edge up to the same slanted line.

6. Make the wolf's ear by turning flap up and over.

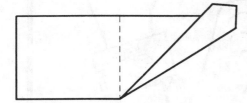

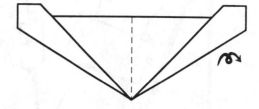

7. Repeat steps on the left side of the paper.

8. Turn the paper over and give the wolf a face.

Native American Bracelet

Goal: To experience an art form of Native Americans.

Materials: Index paper, string, hole punch, felt pens, beads or beans of various sizes and colors, paper punch, string, scissors, glue

Directions: Reproduce the patterns on page 35 onto index paper. This will be used for the bracelet. Decorate the bracelet with felt pens or glue on beads of various sizes and colors. Spray with a clear acrylic finish if desired. Punch a hole at each end of the bracelet and tie it onto the wrist with the string. Bracelets may be cut off from both sides to fit smaller wrists.

Extensions: Make a "silver" bracelet by covering cardboard with aluminum foil. Glue on macaroni to create a pattern. Uncooked macaroni can be dyed by soaking it in a desired food coloring diluted with water. (Adding a little rubbing alcohol helps the macaroni dry more quickly.)

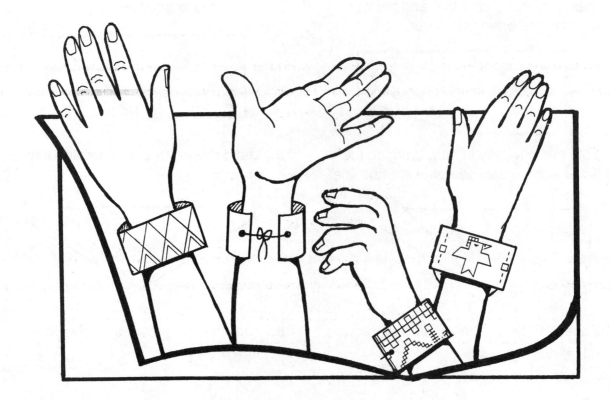

Native American Bracelet Patterns

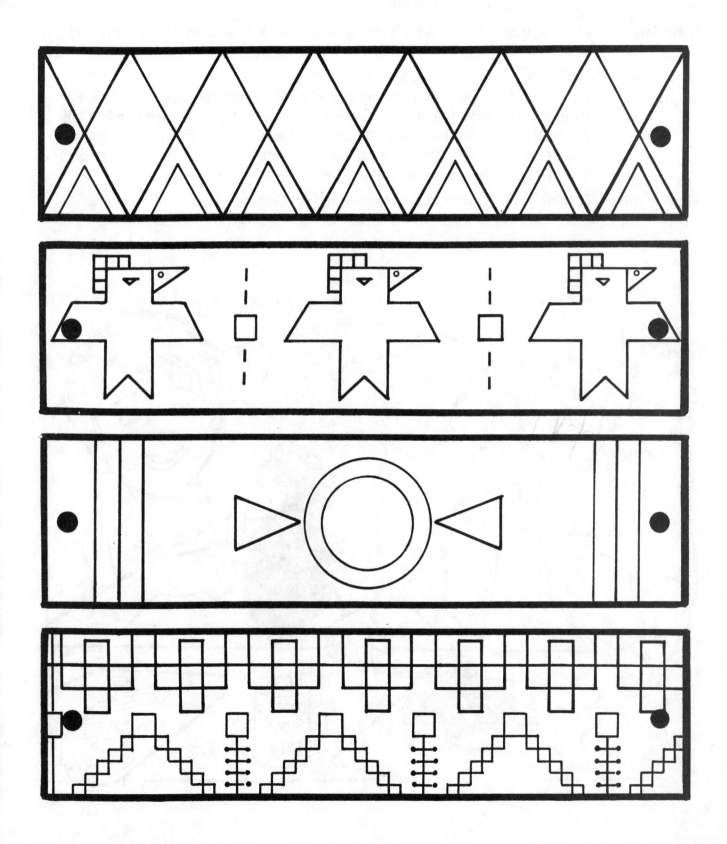

Fish Prints

Goal:　　　　To explore an Oriental art form.

Materials:　　Any flat, whole fish (fresh or plastic), such as flounder or sole; block-printing ink; 5" (13 cm) roller; newspaper; newsprint paper; drawing paper; water; paintbrush

Directions:　Ink fish with block-printing ink, using the roller. Completely cover the fish. Be careful not to apply the ink too thickly. Use brush to cover edges with ink. Lift fish and place inked side down on drawing paper. Cover fish with newspaper and press down with hands, using light pressure. Remove newspaper and lift fish by tail, peeling fish from paper. Let dry and frame.

Extensions:　Display the fish prints in an International Art Gallery.

Native American Sand Painting

Goal: To experience a Native American art form.

Materials: Sand (white and clean) or salt, food coloring, cardboard, small-tipped brushes, books of Native American designs or pattern on page 38, small containers with lids for sand, water, aluminum pie plates, pencils, scissors, glue

Directions: Put a cup (250 mL) of sand into each container, add ¼ cup (60 mL) water with food coloring in it. Mix the sand and colored water together. Strain out extra water and let the sand dry. Do this for each color you need. Draw the desired design on the cardboard. Using the small-tipped brush, apply glue to the cardboard where you prefer a certain color of sand. Sprinkle the sand on the glue and let it dry. Continue until you have finished the entire picture.

Extension: Let children draw a design of their own. Provide sand and glue and allow them to color their designs. Use the sand paintings in an international classroom art gallery.

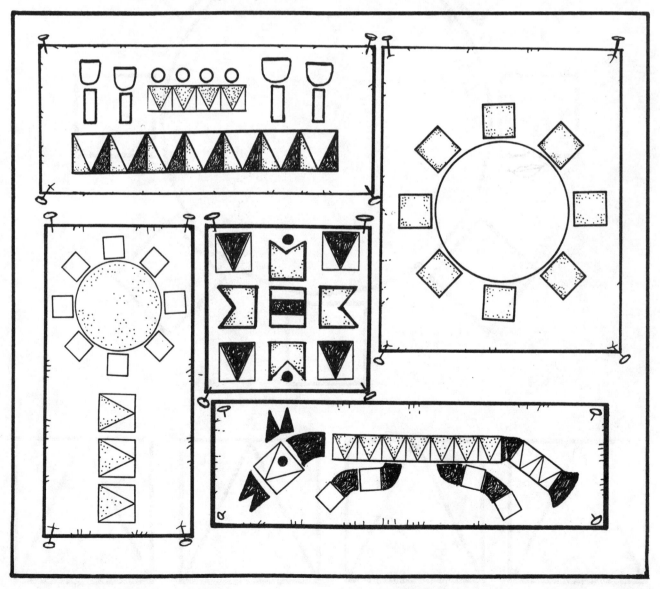

Native American Designs

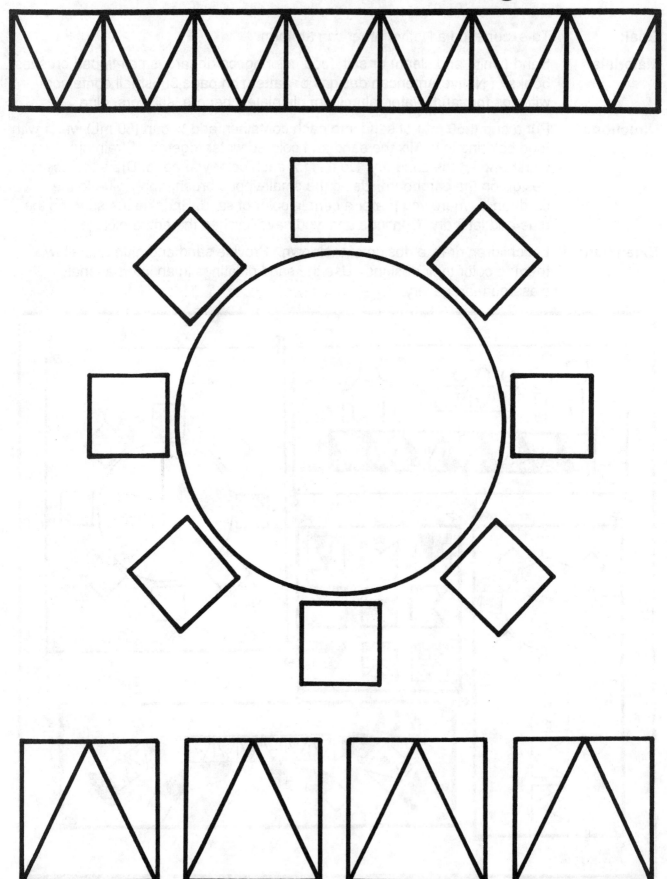

Oriental Lettering and Scroll Painting

Goal: To experience an art form practiced in the Far East.

Materials: Watercolor paints, black ink, fine-tipped paintbrushes, straws, paper, string or yarn, wallpaper scraps

Directions: Before you begin this lesson, have children practice using brushes and straw to design a variety of oriental lettering styles. Take a piece of 11" x 14" (28 cm x 36 cm) watercolor paper on which children will create oriental letterings, as well as pictures—particularly of things found in nature. These should both be done in black only. Paper should be held with the 14" (36 cm) side on top. In the bottom right corner, have children make a 1" x 1" (2.5 cm x 2.5 cm) design, painted in one color only. This is called a "chop" and represents their signature. Fold a strip of paper or colored paper over top of scroll about 1" (2.5 cm) and thread string or yarn through the fold to create a hanger for the scroll. Glue this to the paper to hold it in place.

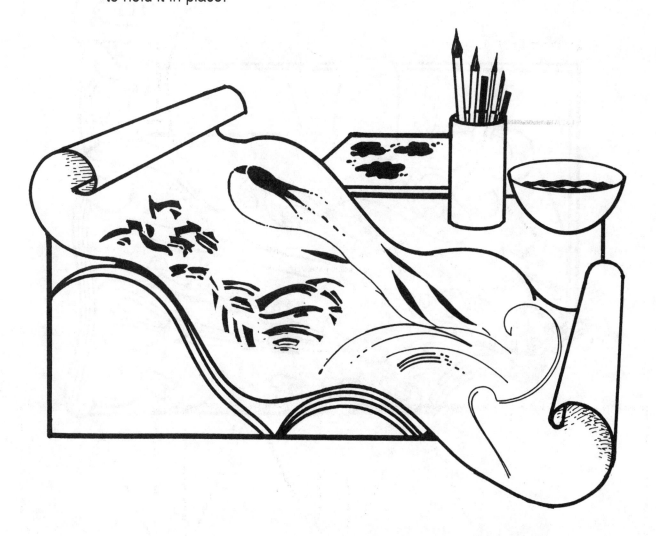

Quilling—Paper Curling

Goal: To experience an art form practiced in Finland and other Scandinavian countries.

Materials: Paper clips, glue, straight pins, paper, pencils, scissor

Directions: Cut out one inch (2.5 cm) strips of paper. Coil paper strips into a variety of sizes. (Younger children may need to be provided with pre-made coils.) Attach coils to each other to create a variety of shapes and designs. (This will resemble grill work.) After the children have practiced with abstract designs, they should connect the coils to form realistic items (i.e. people, animals or scenes).

Extensions: Let children attach the coils to sheets of construction paper to create pictures.

Columbian Weaving

Goal: To practice a form of weaving from Central and South America.

Materials: Cardboard approximately 6" x 9" (15 x 23 cm), string or twine, various colors of yarn, craft sticks, drill

Directions: Cut six notches off the short ends of the cardboard. Wrap string through the notches. Tie off the ends and then begin to weave under and over. Tie off at the end. If children have trouble weaving the yarn through use a craft stick. Drill a hole at one end and thread the yarn through or tie it tightly around the end and let them use the stick to weave.

Extensions: Sew all the pieces of weaving together. Use as a mat or wall hanging in the classroom.

Construction paper strips can be used in place of yarn for weaving.

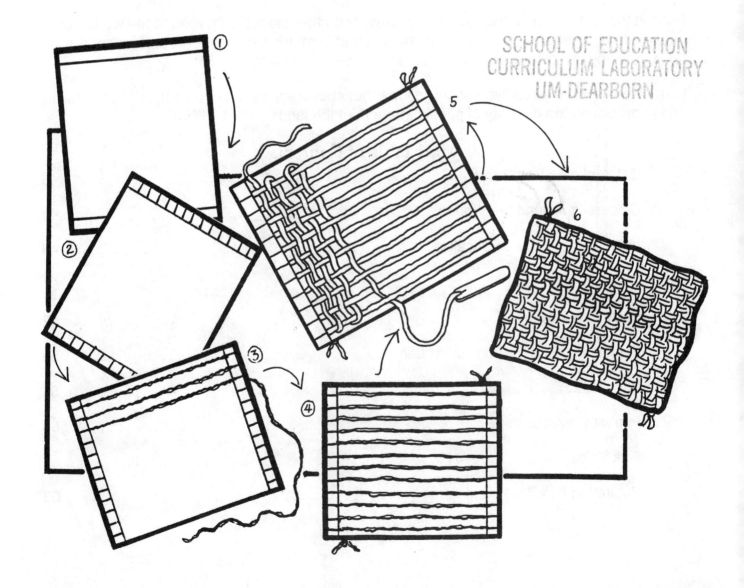

SCHOOL OF EDUCATION
CURRICULUM LABORATORY
UM-DEARBORN

Celebrating International Language Arts

Celebrating International Language Arts, as part of the extended theme *Celebrating Diversity*, will take you and your students on a trip around the world. This unit, rich in experiences for children, focuses on stories, language, and the way people communicate. Start the unit by introducing students to a universal fairy tale—*Cinderella*. Use the bulletin board on pages 43-46 to set the mood for the unit. This is an ongoing bulletin board to which children can contribute as the unit progresses.

Read a Cinderella story, or better still, tell one to your class. Be dramatic in your telling and draw the children in with the richness of the language. Use a world map to show the children where the version of the story you are reading comes from. Ask them to be on the alert for any modern-day movies or books that have a Cinderella theme.

Expand the unit by sharing storybooks, poems, and other stories from around the world. Use puppets to help tell stories. Talk about the fact that communication is an important aspect in understanding our differences, and that people need to learn to listen.

Language arts is an area that not only allows, but encourages student participation in realizing and appreciating the diversity of people throughout the lands.

Mini Table of Contents

Cinderella Bulletin Board

Bulletin Board

Back the bulletin board with brown butcher paper or grocery sacks. Title the bulletin board "Cinderella's Tokens." Reproduce the book cover on page 45 for each student. Reproduce the patterns on pages 44-46. As the various versions of Cinderella are read, let children choose one of the patterns, cut and color it out, and glue it to the book cover. Place the book covers onto the bulletin board. You may wish to add the story chart (page 48) that you are keeping as you read each version of *Cinderella*.

Variations: Give children copies of the book covers and let them draw pictures of their favorite Cinderella. Hang these up on the bulletin board.

Extensions: There are several versions of *Cinderella* on videos. Choose one for your class to watch. After watching the video, make some comparisons between literature and film. Add the information to the story chart.

Bulletin Board Patterns *(cont.)*

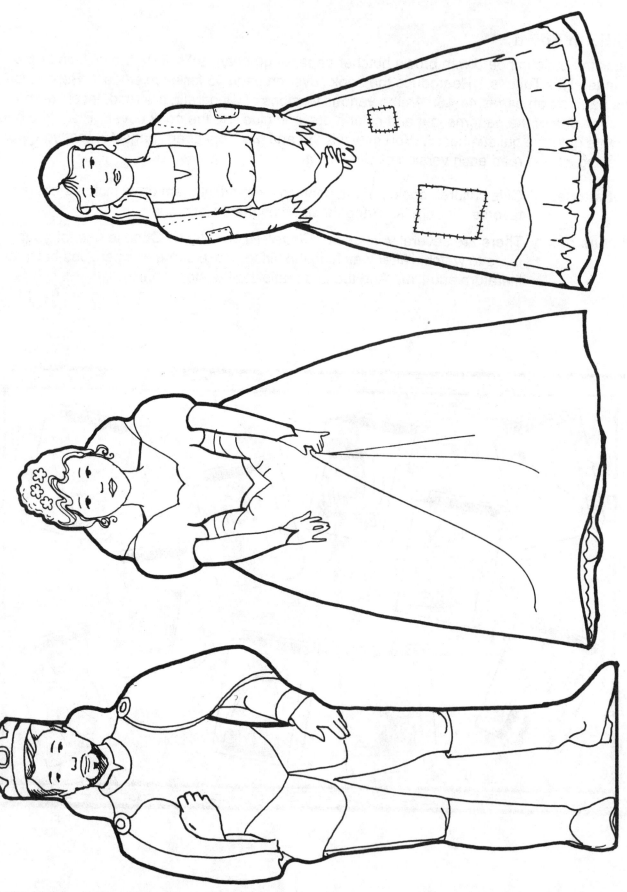

Bulletin Board Patterns *(cont.)*

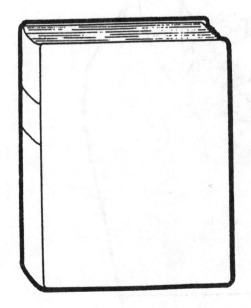

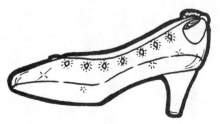

Bulletin Board Patterns *(cont.)*

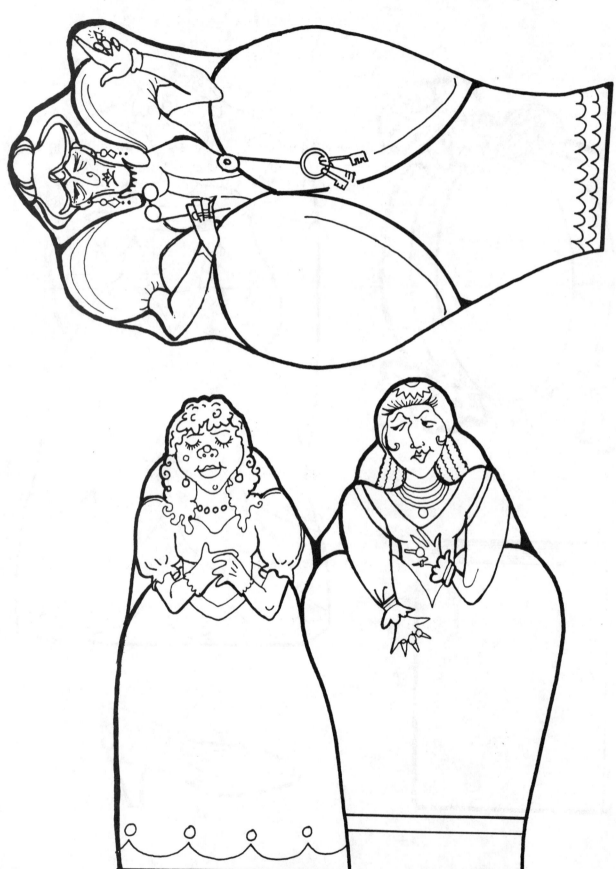

Cinderella Around the World

Goal: To see how the same story is told differently throughout the world.

Materials: Several versions of the Cinderella story, classroom chart

Directions: There are about 100 versions of the Cinderella story from around the world. The most ancient version of the Cinderella story comes from 9th century China. Each week read one version of the Cinderella story. (A suggested list of different versions is given below.) As you read, you may wish to stop at intervals and have children predict what will happen next. Discuss each version of the story and keep a story chart in the room. Choose from the chart on page 48 and compare the stories weekly.

The following versions can be read.

- *Mufaro's Beautiful Daughters* by John Steptoe. Lothrop, Lee, Shepherd, 1987. (An African Folk Tale.)

- *The Rough-Face Girl* by Rafe Martin. Putnam, 1992. (An Algonguin Indian Folk Tale.)

- *The Egyptian Cinderella* by Shirley Climo. Harper Collins, 1992. (An Egyptian Version.)

- *Yeh Shen: A Cinderella Story* retold by Louie Ai-Ling. Putnam, 1988. (A Chinese Version.)

- *Cinderella* by Charles Perrault. Knopf, 1988. (A French Tale.)

- *The Brocaded Slippers and other Vietnamese Tales* by Lynette Dyer Vuong. Harper Collins, 1992. (A Vietnamese Version.)

- *Abadeha: The Philippine Cinderella* by Myrna J. De La Paz. Pazific Queen, 1991. (A Philippine Version.)

- *Vasilissa the Beautiful: A Russian Tale* by Elizabeth Winthrop. Harper Collins, 1991. (A Russian Tale.)

- *Tattercoats* by Margaret Greaves. Crown, 1990. (A British Version.)

- *Moss Gown* by William Hooks. Houghton Mifflin, 1990. (An American Southern Version.)

- *Prince Cinders* by Babette Cole. Putnam, 1992. (A version in which Cinderella is a male.)

Cinderella Story Chart

Cinderella Story Chart			
Version			
Beginning Words			
The Magic			
Royal Character			
Evil Character			
Animal Character			
Special Number			
Lesson			
Ending Words			

Cinderella Story Chart			
Cinderella			
Country			
Young Man			
Helpers			
Messenger			
Token			

An International Food—Pancakes

Goal: To share a story about an international food—pancakes.

Materials: *Pancakes for Breakfast* by Tomie dePaola (HBJ, 1978), page 50 reproduced, pencils

Directions: Share some of the following information about pancakes with your students. Pancakes are believed to be the oldest prepared food. Pounded grain and water, mixed together and cooked on a hot stone may have constituted the first pancakes. Pancakes today are found all over the world. They include French *crepes*, Hungarian *palacintas*, Indian *dosai*, Italian *cannelloni*, Jewish *blintzes*, and Russian *blini*.

Have the children tell you about how they think pancakes are made. Ask them what ingredients are included. Write these on the board.

Then read *Pancakes for Breakfast*. Compare what was used in the story to what they thought went into pancakes.

Use the follow up on page 50. Before children answer the questions talk about question words such as who, what, when, where, why, and how. Have children choose the correct answer and write it on the pancakes.

Extensions: Hold a pancake breakfast. Ask parents to contribute pancake mix, syrup, butter or margarine, juice, and paper goods. (They may even supply the labor!) Use electric frying pans and make pancakes for the children to eat.

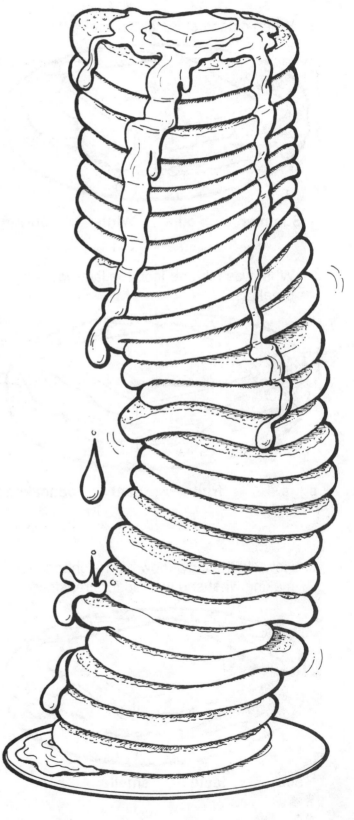

Pancakes for Breakfast

After reading the story *Pancakes for Breakfast* answer the following questions. Choose the answer and write it on the pancake.

1. When did the story take place?

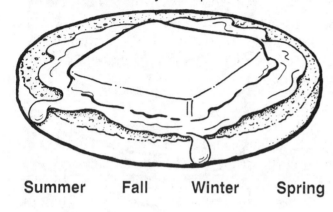

Summer   Fall   Winter   Spring

2. Who kept the lady from enjoying breakfast at her house?

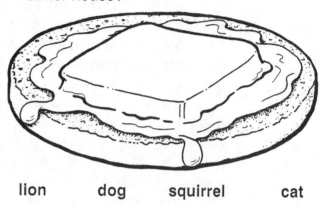

lion   dog   squirrel   cat

3. What was the one food the lady wanted for breakfast?

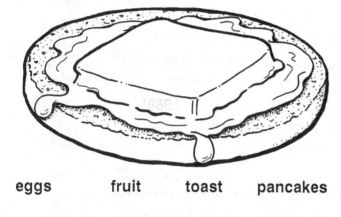

eggs   fruit   toast   pancakes

4. The lady was missing ingredients. Name one.

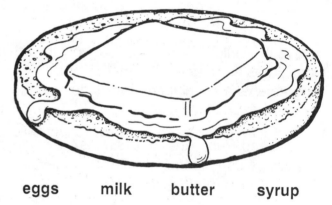

eggs   milk   butter   syrup

5. How did the lady know her neighbors were making what she wanted for breakfast?

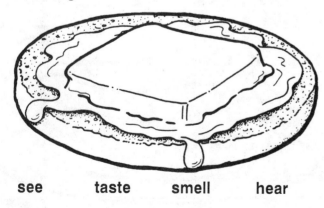

see   taste   smell   hear

6. What do you like to eat on your pancakes?

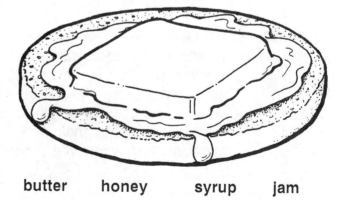

butter   honey   syrup   jam

Quilt Stories

Goal: To share stories about quilts to see the roles they play in people's lives.

Materials: A book that features quilts as part of the story (see list below), construction paper, crayons, tape

Directions: Choose a story that features quilts. Share it with the class. After reading the story ask the children why the quilt was so important to the story. If possible share a patchwork quilt with the students, pointing out the different squares. Many quilts have squares that are made from old items of clothing and may represent an important event in its creator's life.

Talk about story quilts and how they are made to tell a particular story. Let students know they will be making one. Have them, as a class, choose a favorite picture book. Read several stories to the children and then let them vote for the one they would like to create a story quilt for. Give each child an 8" (20 cm) construction-paper square. Have each child choose a scene to illustrate on the square, making sure to include his or her name on the square. Then put the squares together to create a quilt. An inch (2.5 cm) border of construction paper can be placed around the quilt. It can then be exhibited on the wall or can be displayed with the different quilt books and the story it illustrates.

- *The Patchwork Quilt* by Valerie Flournoy. (Dial Books, 1985)
- *The Canada Geese Quilt* by Natalie Kinsey. (Dell, 1992)
- *Sam Johnson and the Blue Ribbon Quilt* by Lisa C. Ernst. (Lothrop, Lee and Shepard, 1983)
- *The Keeping Quilt* by Patricia Polacco. (Simon and Schuster, 1988)
- *The Quilt* by Ann Jonas. (Greenwillow, 1984)
- *The Quilt Story* by Tony Johnston. (Putnam, 1992)
- *The Josefina Story Quilt* by Eleanor Coerr. (Harper Collins, 1989)

Storybook Day

Goal: To share favorite storybooks with each other.

Materials: Favorite storybooks, costumes

Directions: Designate one day as Storybook Day. Send a letter home to parents telling them that on this day children will be asked to share their favorite storybooks with the class. Encourage students to dress up as one of the characters in the storybook. Have children share their books with the class. They may read the story, or tell something about why it is their favorite book.

Extensions:

1. The teacher chooses his or her favorite storybook and shares it with the class. He or she dresses up as a character from the book. This works well in conjunction with a particular area of study or an author you may be highlighting if you choose a corresponding book.

2. Make Storybook Day an ongoing activity. Each month let a few children share their favorites with their classmates.

Exploring Literature from Other Lands

Goal: To improve reading skills and gain a better understanding of literature from other lands.

Materials: Storybooks or anthologies of literature from other countries

Directions: Explore and read literature from other countries to children. Have them discuss and compare similarities and differences from their own culture. Some common themes to watch for and discuss would be heroes, villains, true love, messengers, helpers, and lessons learned. Use a Venn diagram (see below) or a story chart to compare and contrast the stories to help children with this activity.

Extensions:

1. Encourage children to bring in storybooks from other countries that they have at home.

2. Invite parents to read some of these stories to the class.

3. Let children share some of the literature from other lands with older reading buddies.

Venn Diagram

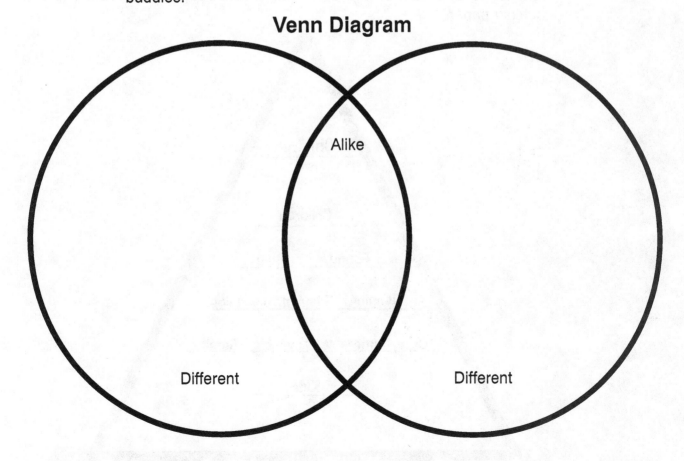

Alike

Different   Different

Poetry

Goal: To write a cinquain about an ideal friend.

Materials: Poetry books, paper, pencil, form on page 55

Directions: Expose students to a variety of poetry by reading several poems to them. Suggestions for poetry anthologies are listed below.

After reading poems, give children an opportunity to write a cinquain. A cinquain is a special type of poem that allows children a successful first experience in writing poetry. The form on page 55 gives directions on how to complete a cinquain.

Have students brainstorm for topics they would like to write a poem about. Either in small groups or as individuals, students can write their cinquains. Younger students may want to dictate their poems to an older child or adult.

Extensions:

1. A book of class poems may be compiled for each child. Poems can be copied on large, lined paper, and accompanied by pictures drawn by the children and then displayed.

2. Students may lay down on brown butcher paper while another child or teacher traces around them. Each child should copy his or her poem onto the butcher paper.

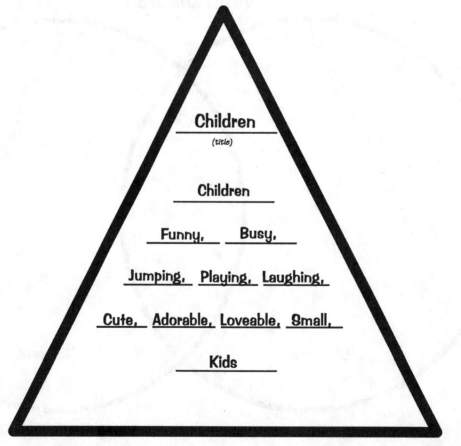

My Cinquain

To write a cinquain do the following:

Line 1:   Write a word that names the subject.

Line 2:   Write two words that describe or define the subject.

Line 3:   Write three action words associated with the subject.

Line 4:   Write four words that show your feelings about the subject.

Line 5:   Write one word that is a synonym for or retells the subject.

Use the lines below to write your poem. Add a title.

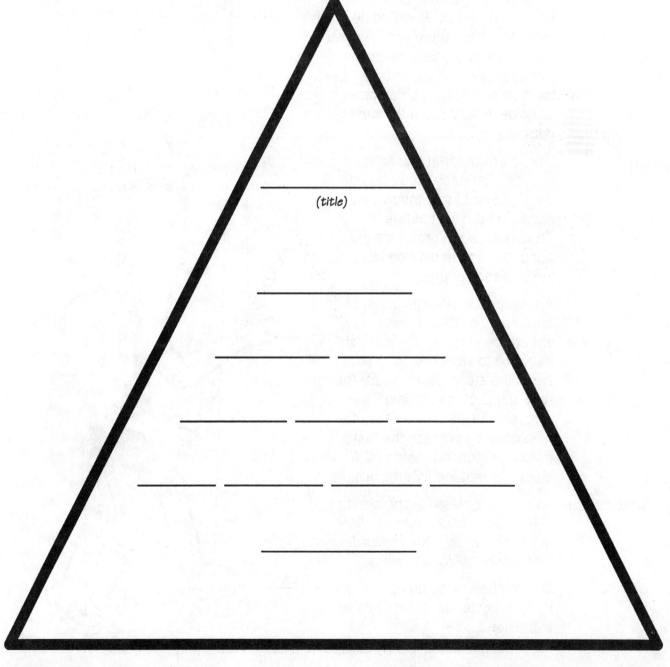

_____
(title)

Puppet Play

Goal: To explore communication skills through puppets.

Materials: Folk tales from around the world, video camera, video tapes, video player, tape recorder, cassette tape, craft sticks, tape or glue, construction paper, old clean socks, small lunch sacks, crayons or markers

Directions: Choose several folk tales from around the world. Read some of them aloud to your class. As you read the stories, tape record them for use at another time. Let the children decide which ones they feel would make the best puppet play.

Divide the children into small groups. Let each group decide on a different story they would like to act out with puppets. Then have each group make puppets. These may be stick, bag, or sock puppets.

An easy puppet stage can be created by putting a towel or sheet over a table. Children sit behind it to work their puppet. Read the story aloud or play the recordings of the stories. The recordings can also be used to help children practice the plays before presenting them to the class. Videotape these activities.

Extensions: As part of a class library, create a videotape section. Allow children to check out any video recording that you have done in class.

Marionettes, puppets operated by strings, can be created as an extension.

Folk Tales

Goal: To understand and create an individual or group folk tale.

Materials: Folk tales from around the world, books, paper, pencils

Directions: Read folk tales from around the world. Talk about how folk tales have always embodied the values of people's cultures. Throughout history they have been used to pass these values from one generation to the next. Explain how folk tales often explain things or teach lessons.

When you have discussed folk tales, brainstorm with students for ideas they may have for their own folk tales. Determine if they are to work alone or as a group. If they work as a group, the members need to agree on the plot. They may write folk tales telling how or why something came to be. Younger children may do this as a group with a teacher or an older student serving as recorder.

Extensions: Children can read their folk tales to one another as part of sharing time or opening activities.

SCHOOL OF EDUCATION
CURRICULUM LABORATORY
UM-DEARBORN

Illustrating Folk Tales

Goal: To use art to illustrate folk tales from other lands.

Materials: Paper, pens, crayons, colored markers, paint

Directions: After completing their own folk tales (page 57) students may illustrate them using a variety of art media. Students who have participated in group stories should decide what portion of their stories they want to illustrate and then each member of the group should complete those illustrations.

Compile the stories into a classroom book. Put the booklet into the class or school library for all to enjoy.

Extensions: Have students create frames for their illustrations. Have them design a simple pattern that would be representative of a culture or a country around the world. Have them look at pictures of art work or clothing for ideas.

Celebrating International Music and Movement

Throughout the world children, music, and movement go together. Music and movement are an integral part of cultures worldwide.

Start this unit by giving children the opportunity to listen to music from around the world. Get some recordings of various types of ethnic music. The public library is usually an excellent source for this. As children listen, have them focus on the sounds that may not sound familiar to them. Encourage them get up and dance. Give them rhythm instruments, either commercially-made or homemade to keep time to the music or place streamers in their hands to dance with.

Set up the Jump Rope Bulletin Board and teach the children some jump-rope rhymes. Let children share them in class.

Show some music videos that are appropriate to the unit of study. Include some with familiar music. Folk music is often sung by children's musicians. Public libraries and children's book stores may be a resource.

Have fun with this unit. Children, music, and movement are a great combination. Let them experience the joy that diverse music and movement can bring them.

Mini Table of Contents

Bulletin Board

Jump Rope

Using a real jump rope, outline the board. Start the word Jump Rope with a real jump rope. On large cards or construction paper, write other movement words such as jumping, leaping, hopping, or bouncing. Attach to the bulletin board.

As an activity, have the children stand at their seats or on the rug. Point to and read one of the words on the bulletin board. Have the children react physically to the movement. As an alternative, have a child choose a word and demonstrate it for the class.

Jump Rope

Goal: To participate in a physical activity enjoyed the world over.

Equipment: Jump rope, jump rope rhymes (page 67)

Directions: Tell children they are about to participate in a universal game. Ask them to think about a game that might be played around the world that requires only one piece of equipment. If no one guesses, tell them they are about to play jump rope. Jump rope is also called skipping rope. It is an easy game to play. It can be played by one child or by many. Children all around the world jump to rhythmic beats and rhymes. Have the children share some of the rhymes that they are familiar with and then share some of those given in this activity. Let them learn some from the various countries.

Jump Rope Rhymes

Teach some of these jump rope rhymes from around the world. Clap the rhythms out. As children take turns jumping, let them recite the words.

The rope is turned very fast in this rhyme found in France, Vietnam, and Canada.

O! The lettuce!

When it grows up,

We will eat it:

With oil and vinegar.

From Australia comes this humorous rhyme.

A rabbit has a shiny nose

I'll tell you why, my friend:

Because her little powder puff

Is on the other end.

This rhyme from Greece tells about the joy of an outdoor celebration.

Skipping fun

Everywhere,

But skipping rope is double-fun

In the open air.

In this rhyme from Kenya, the jumper pretends to be jelly and then sausage by wiggling around while jumping.

Jelly on the plate, jelly on the plate

Wiggle, woggle, wiggle, woggle

Jelly on the plate.

Sausage in the pan, sausage in the pan

Turn it around, turn it around

Sausage in the pan.

This rhyme is recited in many English-speaking countries.

I saw Esau

Sitting on a seesaw

And Esau saw I saw him

Though Esau saw I saw him saw

Still Esau went on sawing.

How many Esaus in that?

(The answer is none.)

This is a traditional nursery rhyme heard both in England and the United States that has been used for skipping rope for generations.

Intry, mintry, cutry corn

Appleseed and apple thorn.

Wire, brier, limber, lock,

Twelve geese in a flock.

One flew east, one flew west,

One flew over the cuckoo's nest.

Instruments Around the World

Goal: To provide an opportunity for students to recognize instruments from around the world.

Materials: Worksheet (page 64), scissors, glue, crayons

Directions: Many cultures are known for their own musical instruments which are unique to their cultures. Have children look at the pictures on page 64. Help them identify the instruments. (See the key below.) Have them cut the labels out and glue them to the instrument. They may choose to color the pictures.

Extensions: Find recordings of some of the instruments listed. Play the recordings and let children guess which instruments they are hearing.

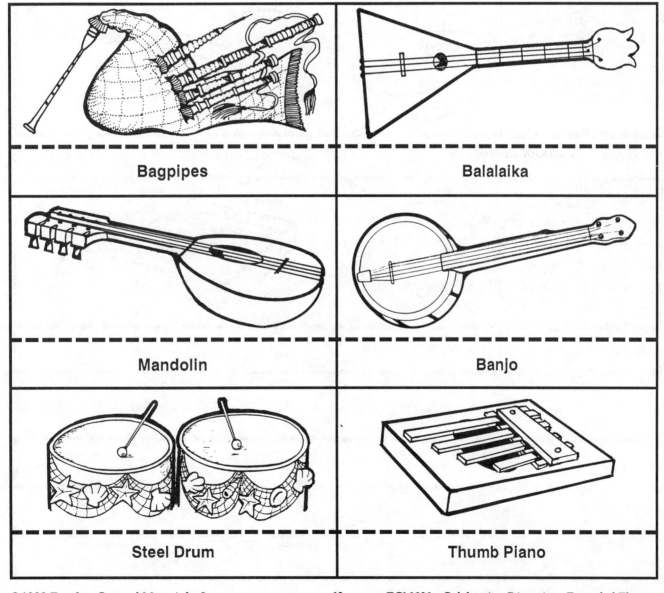

Bagpipes	Balalaika
Mandolin	Banjo
Steel Drum	Thumb Piano

Instruments Around the World *(cont.)*

There are many kinds of instruments found around the world. Match the name of the instrument with the picture. Cut out the answer and glue it in the box, then color the picture.

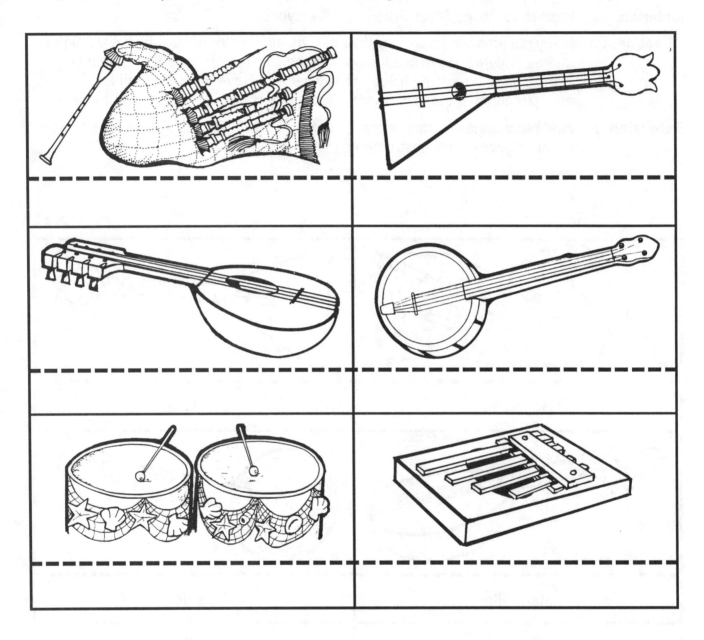

Banjo	Balalaika
Mandolin	Steel Drum
Thumb Piano	Bagpipes

Native American Rattle

Goal: To give children an opportunity to create an important Native American instrument.

Materials: Two paper cups, pebbles, masking tape or colored plastic, felt pens

Directions: Explain to children that rattles were very important to the Native Americans and they used many different types. Medicine men shook special rattles in ceremonies and healing rituals. Rattles were used as musical instruments during dances and as background for singers.

Have children make a rattle. To make the rattle, decorate the cups and put the pebbles inside. Tape the cups together and shake.

Extensions: Make other types of rattles. One can be made from a cardboard tube. Tape one end of the tube (paper towel) closed. Place beans inside. Shake to determine sound and add more until the desired sound is attained. Tape the open end closed. Decorate with marking pens.

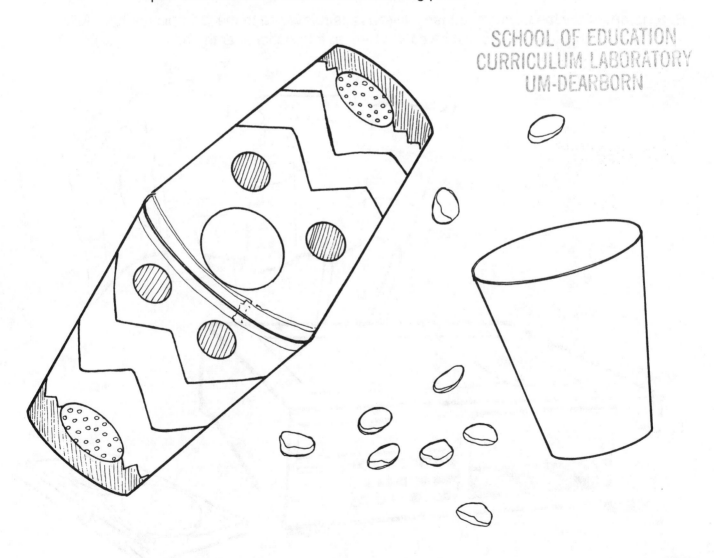

Anthems from Other Lands

Goal: To experience a variety of music that represents countries from around the world.

Materials: Recordings and printed copies of a variety of national anthems (available at local libraries). Some to include are: "The Star Spangled Banner"—United States; "God Save the Queen"—England; "Marseillaise"—France; "Deutschland Uber Alles"—Germany; "O Canada"—Canada.

Directions: Have children listen to a variety of national anthems. As they listen, explain that national anthems are official patriotic songs of individual nations. They are a musical representation of a country and are played at official and public gatherings. They are often marches or hymns. As students listen point out on a map which country's anthem they are listening to. What is the music like? Is it loud or soft? What do they think the music might stand for? Tell them that national anthems are often written to honor a national hero or an important event in the country's history. Ask them to make connections in the type of music they hear.

Extension: Play the Olympic anthem. Discuss its relevance to the Olympic games. Ask children why it could be considered an international anthem.

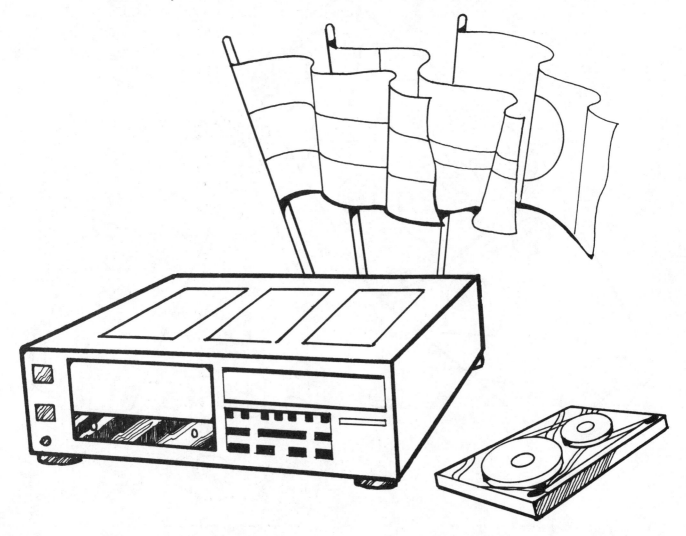

Songs from Around the World

Goal: To build a cultural awareness through a variety of songs.

Materials: Elementary song texts

Suggested song titles collected by the students or songs from the following books would be helpful:

American Folk Songs for Children by Ruth Seeger (Doubleday, 1980)

Voices of the World by Irving Wolfe (Follett, 1980)

Making Music Your Own by Harold Youngberg (Silver Burdett, 1986)

Exploring Music by Eunice Boardman (Holt, Rhinehart, Winston, 1971)

Music and You by Barbara Straton (Macmillan, 1988)

Directions:

Part One: Discuss the history and origin of songs found in your elementary song text. Sing songs and have students accompany the music with their own instruments.

Part Two: Have students collect a variety of songs and song titles which are favorites of their families or which represent their family heritage. Ask parents to send in words and music. Use the family song titles to create a class collage or a class songbook. Let the children decorate the cover of the songbook.

Composers

Goal: To learn about famous composers from around the world.

Materials: Books about composers around the world, recordings by famous composers

Directions: Talk about what a composer does. Ask children to name any composers of whom they may have heard. Add to their list from the list below. Ask them what important information they should know about each composer. Help them to find some of that information by using encyclopedias or other research books. Have students choose one composer to research. Encourage them with parents help, to find a recording of the composer's music and bring it in to share with the class.

Extensions: Locate a local composer and have him/her visit your school. University and college music departments may be a good source of composers.

- Johann Sebastian Bach
- George Frederick Handel
- Franz Joseph Haydn
- Wolfgang Amadeus Mozart
- Ludwig von Beethoven
- Franz Schubert
- Robert Schumann
- Clara Wieck Schumann
- Johannes Brahms
- Peter Ilich Tchaikovsky
- Claude Debussy
- Igor Stravinsky
- Carl Orff
- Ruth Crawford Seeger
- Aaron Copland
- Leonard Bernstein
- John Lennon
- Paul McCartney
- Duke Ellington

Jazz

Goal: To become familiar with American jazz; to begin to see the relationship between West African music and American jazz.

Materials: Jazz recordings, paper, crayons

Directions: Choose several different jazz recordings to play for your class. (Public libraries often have recordings available.) Play them for the children. As children listen, have them try to softly tap out the rhythm they are hearing. Ask if it is easy to keep time to the music and if every song has the same rhythm.

Explain that jazz has its beginnings in African music which features steady rhythm, spontaneous improvisation, and lively dialogue similar to that found in jazz today. Jazz actually grew out of the funerals of Black slaves. The only time they were allowed to sing in public was at funerals. On the way to the cemetery the music would be slow and sad, but on the way back it would often be joyful. Drums were not allowed but the slaves often improvised. The early slaves kept American jazz alive.

Ask children what they hear in the jazz music. How does it sound compared to other music they have heard? Do they recognize any instruments? (They may hear drums, piano, guitar, bass, or a vibraphone.)

After listening to the music, have children design an album cover for some of the recordings heard. When children are through, play some of the songs again. Ask children to hold up their covers as the song it represents is played.

Global Hopscotch

Goal: To learn a simple game and its simple variation.

Materials: Shoe polish (if indoors), chalk or paint (if outdoors), laggers—rocks, stones, small chains

Directions: Ask children how many of them know how to play hopscotch. Find out if they all know the same version. Then explain that hopscotch is an international game, played around the world. It has many variations. Using the directions below, demonstrate a version called *klassa* from Poland for the class.

In *klassa* children imagine that they are hopping in and out of grades (*klassa*) in school. Draw the hopscotch diagram on the playground with chalk. Throw a lagger into box 1. Jump into box 1 with both feet. Pick up your lagger. Now jump into the rest of the boxes, 2 through 7 in order and them back again. Jump out. Throw your lagger into box 2, then jump into box 1. Then jump into box 2, pick up your lagger, and complete the game all the way to box 7 and back again. Continue to play tossing the lagger into each box in order. The winner is the first one to play all the way to box 7 without touching a line or missing a box when throwing the lagger.

Extensions: The book *Hopscotch Around The World* by Mary D. Lanford (Morrow, 1992) is a wonderful collection of all types of hopscotch. Choose a variation of this universal game and have a hopscotch tournament.

Klassa Diagram

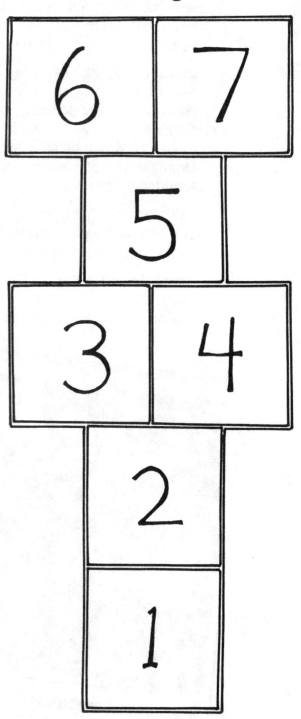

Bowling

Goal: To show how a game has changed and developed through the years, yet stayed basically the same.

Materials: Empty, clean milk cartons, construction paper, scissors, glue or tape, rubber ball

Directions: Before beginning share some history of the sport or game of bowling. It has been found in Egyptian tombs from 5300 B.C. The game was used in a modified form in the Middle Ages to prove guilt or innocence. The accused bowled a ball at one pin about 60 feet (18 m) away. If it knocked over the pin, the accused was innocent; if not, guilty. The game of bowling came to the United States with the early Dutch settlers in New York. The game was 9 pins to 10 pins, back to 9, then back to 10 pins. The shape of the pins has changed, as has the ball and the distance of the lane, but the game is basically the same.

For this activity, students will use milk cartons as bowling pins and knock them down with the ball. Cover milk cartons with construction paper. Line the cartons up several feet away from the children. See the diagram. Mark a starting line. Use a rubber ball and let them knock the pins down.

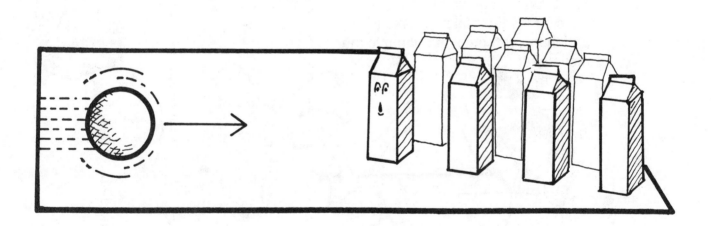

The Tarantella

Goal: To help children develop an appreciation for the dance and music of another country—Italy; to dance the tarantella.

Materials: Recording of the tarantella (The cassette or compact disk of *All the Best from Italy*, Volume 3 features "La Danza Tarantella." It is available at record stores.) record, tape or compact disc players, tambourine (optional)

Directions: Share the story behind the tarantella. It gets its name from the city of Taranto in Italy. It is believed that the people danced this dance as a cure for a tarantula bite. Therefore the dance is very light and lively.

Teach the basic step. Begin by stepping to the right on your right foot. Hop on it. Repeat this basic step on your left side. Practice this. When it feels comfortable, do the step-hop on the right, and then swing your left foot over the right. Repeat on the other side. Now add arm movements. Hold arms straight up over the head. When moving to the left, bend them a little to the left; when moving to the right bend a little to the right. There are many variations for performing this dance. Let children try these with partners. They may move forward and backward or hop on one foot. Let them try some heel-toe movements, runs, or skips.

Tambourines can be used while dancing the tarantella. Shake them, and then bang them in rhythm to the movement.

Tinikling

Goal: To teach cooperation and rhythm in an interesting, challenging way.

Materials: Bamboo sticks or broom handles, small boards 12" x 3" (30 cm x 8 cm); music is optional

Directions: Let children try this dance that is often done by Filipino, Indonesian, and Polynesian children. The dance is an imitation of the long-legged tinikling bird which picks its way through grass stems and fallen trees. The sticks are clicked together on the small boards.

Bamboo Hop Instructions

Terms

TS—Tinikling Step

BH—Bamboo Hop

D—Double

1—Direction

L—Left

R—Right

B—Boy

G—Girl

Patterns

Dance Pattern: A pattern consists of the repeating of a basic step, or form of a basic step, with a special turn done to the first 24 beats of the music, and then the same in the opposite direction with a special ending for the last 24 beats.

Poles Pattern

Beat 1—strike together

Beat 2—strike boards (poles 1 foot (30 cm) apart)

Beat 3—strike boards (poles 1 foot (30 cm) apart)

(repeat 16 times)

Basic Steps

When the poles are apart you're working inside. When the poles are together you're working outside.

Tinikling Step (TS)

Left: Hop once on your left foot outside the poles, followed by two hops inside the poles on the same spot first by the right foot, then by the left. (LRL—3 beats).

Right: Same as left, except with the opposite feet (RLR—3 beats).

Bamboo Hop (BH)

Left: Same as Tinikling Step except the two hops inside the poles are done on the same foot (LRR—3 beats).

Right: Same as Tinikling Step except the two hops inside the poles are done on the same foot (RLL—3 beats).

Limbo-Dancing:
A West Indies Dance

Goal: To challenge children to move in an awkward, but fun way to perform a task (moving under the bar).

Materials: Two high-jump standards, a bamboo pole or high jump crossbar, music is optional.

Directions: The limbo is a challenging dance-type activity that comes from the West Indies. The object is to bend/lean backwards from the waist and move under the bar pole. The bar is then lowered. Students are eliminated for not making it underneath, touching the pole, having parts of the body touch the floor, or not going under the bar the correct way. The unacceptable ways to do the limbo-bending are going under, ducking under, and touching the ground. Adding lively music, preferably from the West Indies, will keep the game moving.

Extensions: Set up two limbo poles and form two teams. The team who has the most members still playing at the end is the winner.

Celebrating International Social Studies

Customs, the way we do things, how we interact with each other, these are all part of social studies. Since the use of media allows us to view many diverse cultures, it is becoming increasingly important for us to understand customs around the world.

Use the activities in Celebrating International Social Studies as a way to find out more about the world. Start with the obvious, a world map. Follow the directions for the bulletin board on page 76, and find out where students' ancestors hail from. Extend into a math activity and see how many people came from the same or different areas of the world.

Mini Table of Contents

Bulletin Board Ideas

Put up a world map (page 142). Title it "We Are From All Over the World." Reproduce the form below. Have children take it home and have their families help them find out where their ancestors came from. Use colored push pins, names, labels, or flags to indicate where these places are on the map. Colored yarn leading from a student's name to a country may also be used.

Note: Consider different family make-ups including foster and adopted children. Give parents the option of not having their child participate.

Extensions: Family colors or flags may be designed, copied, and colored before using. Create charts or graphs for the map to indicate the number of people and their country of origin.

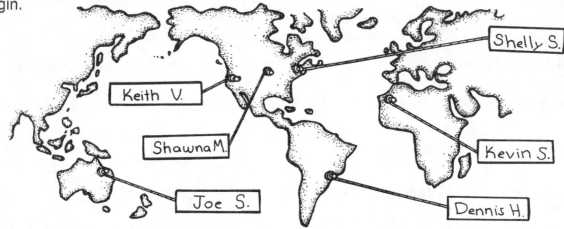

Dear_____,

Can you help me find out where our family came from? Would you write down the countries from around the world that members of our families lived in? We will be using the information on a class bulletin board.

Thanks!

_____

Your student

New Year's Celebrations Around the World

Goal: To research and understand how people from other countries celebrate the New Year.

Materials: Encyclopedias, reference books, contacting family members for interviews

Directions: Students will research a New Year's tradition common to their own ethnic background or one of their own choice. Note: Not all New Year's celebrations take place on January 1st. Children may wish to find out about and share some of these. They may talk about them or write a story for the class. If food is included they may wish to include a recipe and food.

Extensions: Explain about New Year's resolutions. They give people an opportunity to try again. Engage the class in a discussion about what might be some resolutions they would make and keep. Ask students to make one or two resolutions. Have them write their resolutions down, put them in their desks, and refer to them throughout the year.

A Dragon for the Chinese New Year

Goal: To understand the meaning of the Chinese New Year and the significance of the dragon and other animals of the Chinese calendar.

Materials: Dragon pattern (pages 79 and 80), markers, paints (various colors), paintbrushes, scissors, computer paper edges, glue, crepe paper streamers, different kinds of paper such as silver wallpaper, candy wrappers, tissue paper

Directions: The Chinese New Year is celebrated in late January or early February in many Chinese communities. It changes because the Chinese year is based on a lunar calendar. In preparation for celebration, houses are cleaned, new clothes are purchased, special foods are prepared, and the colors of joy, red and orange are seen everywhere. In many communities parades are held featuring the Chinese dragon. The dragon was considered sacred and was a symbol of the Chinese emperor. It stood for strength and goodness. Reproduce the dragon head on page 79 and the segments of the body on page 80. Reproduce as many body segments as needed to make your dragon very long. You may wish to enlarge all the pieces. Have children collect and bring in different materials. Have them use the materials to create scales. Glue them to the dragon. Children can use paint and markers to add to the design. Put the dragon up as a decoration in your classroom.

Extensions: Read the book *Gung Hay Fat Choy* by June Behrens. (Childrens Press, 1982) to your class. This book with its colorful photographs will explain the importance of the Chinese New Year celebration in the Chinese community.

Dragon Pattern

Reproduce the head of the dragon onto index paper. Cut out and color.

Dragon Pattern *(cont.)*

Reproduce as many segments of the dragon body as desired. Have students make scales for the dragon by gluing pieces of paper on the body segments or drawing or coloring. Attach pieces to each other and then attach the body to the head.

A Straw Man from Ecuador

Goal: To experience a different way of celebrating the New Year.

Materials: Old shirts, pants, hats, shoes, needle, thread, straw, brown paper, staples, markers, and newspaper

Directions: Ask children how they celebrate New Year's. Let them know that in other countries it is not celebrated the same. Tell them about the New Year in Ecuador. This involves the whole family. December 31st is called *Año Viejo* which means "old year." Ecuadorean families create a scarecrow using old clothes. They write a will for him that lists everyone's faults. At midnight they read it, and then they burn the scarecrow. Along with the scarecrow everyone's faults disintegrate. Explain to children that they will have a similar experience.

Have children trace themselves twice on brown paper. Using paint and markers, color clothes on their shapes. Cut out shapes, staple together, and stuff them with newspaper. These will represent the Straw Man of Ecuador. He represents the old year, the *Año Viejo*. Explain what a last will and testament is. Students then write a last will and testament for the old straw man, of things they would like to change and improve upon in the coming year.

Extensions: Students dictate or write a story about their Straw Man.

World Flag

Goal: To incorporate the values of peace, truth, honesty, and unity found in the world nation of the future.

Materials: Drawing paper, crayons—red, blue, black, yellow and green, markers

Directions: Flags are usually made of cloth. They are symbols for things such as countries, groups, or organizations. National flags form an important group of flags. The following terms apply to flags:

>*badge or device*—emblem or design on the flag
>
>*canton*—the upper corner of a flag next to the staff; a special design appears here such as the field of stars on the United States flag.
>
>*field*—the background of a flag
>
>*fly*—the free end of a flag; this is farthest from the staff
>
>*ground*—background of a flag
>
>*hoist*—the part of the flag closet to the staff
>
>*staff*—flagpole

Before beginning this activity, share some of the flag terminology. Ask children to think about these parts of the world flag they are about to create. There are two options for this lesson—individual or group.

Individual: Using pencil and paper, individual students design what they feel would represent a world flag.

Group: The group brainstorms shapes, symbols, and designs which could possibly be used for a world flag. As a group, they design a flag on large paper.

Whether this activity is done individually or as a group, every flag should use the colors red, blue, black, yellow, and green. This is due to the fact that at least one of these colors is found in every country's flag.

Extensions: Make copies of some of the flags of the countries around the world and combine them to create an International Flag Display.

Travel Log

To understand what goes into planning a trip to another country; to build an understanding of a particular geographical location, as well as some of the social, cultural, and physical uniqueness found in this country.

.ls: My Favorite Place (page 84), travel brochures

.ions: Before beginning this lesson, collect as many travel brochures from around the world as possible. Encourage children to bring them in too. Let children spend some time looking at these travel brochures. Help them discover what information is covered about the countries that people can visit, what type of pictures are included, and what might be needed to take a trip. Let the students choose a place which interest them. Using information from the travel brochures, travel magazines, books, encyclopedias, or their own travel experiences, have them complete the travel log. The pages can be put together to form a Class Travel Guide for students to look at for ideas about places they want to visit some day.

Extensions: The travel brochures can extend the bulletin board on page 76. Put them up on the board near the map and connect each by yarn to the country or area it describes.

My Travel Log

My favorite place is

Victoria Canada

Some typical clothing might look like

Some foods are

The weather there is usually

Overcast

Sam Brown

World Traveler

My Favorite Place

My Travel

Log

Some foods are

The weather there is usually

World Traveler

My favorite place is

Some typical clothing might look like

Pack Your Suitcase

Goal: To discover information about a particular country and to understand what would be necessary to bring on a trip to a foreign country.

Materials: Suitcase, book bags, duffel bags, brown paper bags, cardboard boxes, worksheet (page 86)

Directions: This lesson would be most effective if it followed the lesson on travel logs and the children remained with the same country they had already researched.

There are three options for this lesson:

1. Children may bring to school a suitcase or bag to use or they may design one from a paper bag or box. They will pack at home what they feel they would need and bring these to school to share with the group.

2. They may fill their bag or box with what they will need written on slips of paper or colored as pictures. These words or pictures can then be pulled from the bag and shared with the group.

3. Reproduce the worksheet. Students may color pictures or write words of what they would pack in their "suitcases." These can be shared and displayed around the room.

Pack Your Suitcase *(cont.)*

Write or draw what is inside your suitcase.

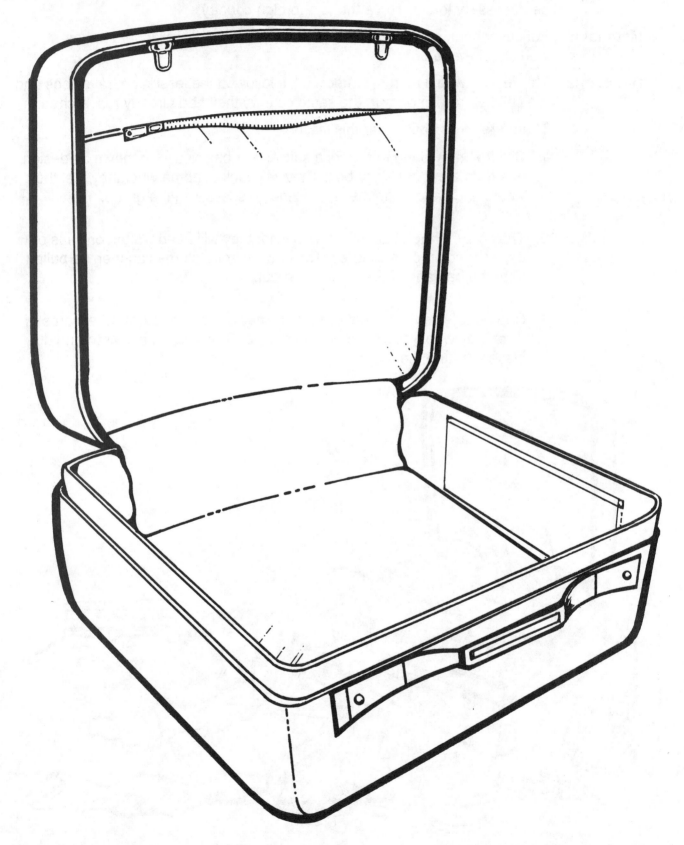

Make a Passport

Goal: To develop an understanding of what a passport is and why it is necessary.

Materials: Student copies of a passport (page 88)

Directions: In order to travel to other countries, a passport is a necessary travel document. A passport identifies the person whose name is on it as a citizen of the country that issued it. It also asks that the person carrying it be given a safe passage through the country.

Have students create a passport for themselves. They may need some help from home to collect the information that is required. Have them fill out the information and either draw a picture or provide a photograph.

Extensions: Passports are not necessary for travel in every country. Find out which do not require passports, but what is required for entry.

Passport Cover

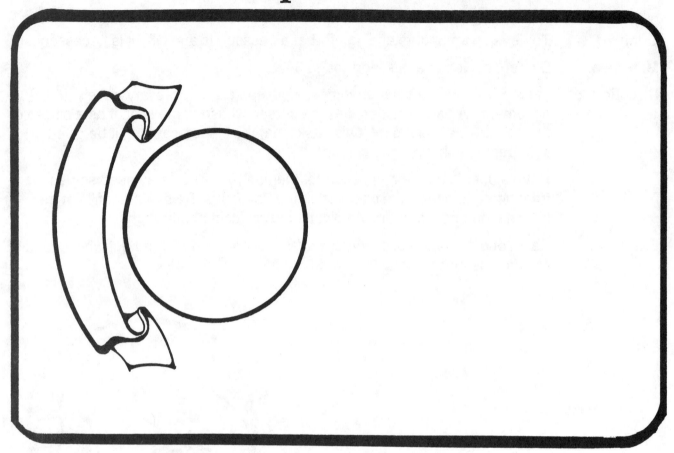

Photo

This passport is
issued to:

_____
(name)

Issue Date:

_____
(Date)

Birthdate: _____

Place of Birth: _____

Map-Making

Goal: To discover why maps are important.

Materials: Brown mural paper, crayons, markers, paint

Directions: Talk about the directions: North, South, East, West. Point them out on a map. Try some of the following activities to reinforce them:

- Have children stand up. Choose a direction and tell them to face that way.

- Stand in the middle of the room. Point out various items in the classroom. Ask which direction the items are from where you are pointing.

- Use masking tape or chalk and draw a huge compass on the school yard. Label the directions. Send groups of students off in the direction you designate.

- Take children for a walk around the school or neighborhood. Let them determine the points of interests. On returning to class, have them work together to create a mural map showing the location of points of interest. Make sure they place a compass on the map.

Extensions: Give the map to another class. Ask the class to follow the students' map. Have them let you know if the map was easy to follow.

Map Your Heritage

Goal: To physically represent countries from your ethnic heritage.

Materials: Markers, crayons, pencils, paper, maps

Directions: Students, after researching their family heritage, construct maps of the countries which are in their family's background. Have them use the information brought from home to help create the bulletin board. (See page 76.)

Either provide maps of the country the children need or a world map for them to color. Small pin flags representing themselves may be used.

Extensions: Use chalk to draw an outline of a world map on the school playground. For each continent use different colored chalk. Label each. Draw the map as large as possible. If there is room let the children walk around the world and stand in the continent that best represents their heritage. Or let each child write his or her name in that continent.

Another Country

Goal: To discover what another country is like and draw comparisons to America.

Materials: Books on a variety of countries, drawing and writing paper

Directions: Choose several books to read to children about the United States and countries around the world. Before reading, inform the children of what information they should be listening for (foods, games, or schools, etc.). After reading the books, make a Venn diagram with the children. As they call out the similarities and differences between the country where the story takes place and America, record them on a large chart.

Extensions: Make this an ongoing project. Keep the Venn diagram chart in the classroom; and, as books are read through the year, add to it.

Occupations

Goal: To foster an awareness of occupations so students can begin thinking about what they might like to be.

Materials: Encyclopedias, books, interviews

Directions: At home, have students make a list of the occupations of people in their family. In class, make a class list. Discuss various occupations. Each child should choose an occupation of interest and illustrate himself or herself at the job. Have children write or dictate a few sentences telling why they might enjoy this job. Invite parents to come in and speak about what they do. Encourage children to ask questions.

Extensions: Provide magazines, scissors, paper, and glue. Children can work together to create small group collages on the careers of parents in general, or of the people who have come in to talk to them. Jobs can be in a specific category such as Helping Careers, Careers in Education, or Careers in Agriculture. The collages can be displayed in the classroom or sent to speakers as thank you gifts.

Celebrating International Expression

What we say, what we wear, and how we represent ourselves, all are a form of expression. Throughout the world people have different ways of expressing themselves.

In some countries it is permissible to eat with one's fingers, while in others one would never think to do that. Public ceremonies that mark birthdays or coming of age vary throughout the world. Clothing, hats, and jewelry are a major way in which we express ourselves; language also plays a major role. These all vary in different countries. The uniqueness in our greetings, either in the way we say "hello" or shake hands, also plays a part in expression.

Set up a bulletin board that shows a "Wheel of Fashion." Patterns are provided on page 95 for hats that can be enlarged and used, but pictures from magazines, student drawings, or authentic items can be substituted. Explain that this is only one way that people around the world express themselves.

We all have a need to express ourselves, and the needs may be fulfilled in different ways. But it is this very sameness for doing things, yet doing them so diversely, that allows us to celebrate international expression.

Mini Table of Contents

Bulletin Board Ideas

To create this bulletin board you will need several long strips of construction paper. Begin by backing the bulletin board with construction paper or wall paper. On each strip write the name of a country. Enlarge the hat patterns on page 95. Color and cut out. Use the names of the countries to create spokes in a wheel. Create the wheel shape by using yarn to form a circle. Pin the appropriate hat next to the country. Title the board "Wheel of Hats." Use it to introduce International Hat Day (page 96).

Variation: Back the bulletin board with a large world map and hang the Wheel of Hats on it.

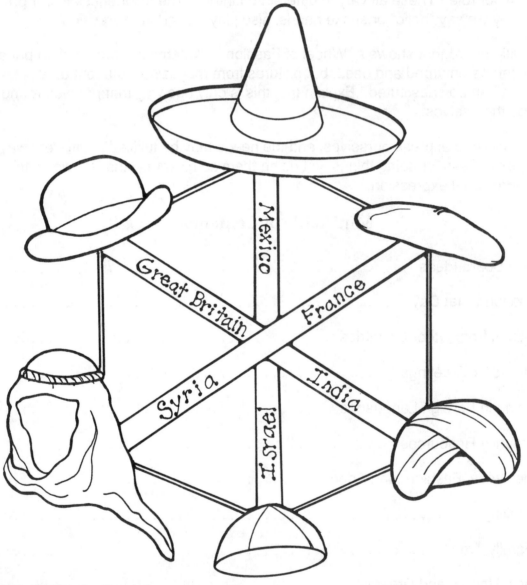

Greeting Bulletin Board

Using construction paper, cut out various sizes, shapes, and colors. On each shape write a greeting in a different language and tell which language it is. (See page 97 for greetings in other languages.) Arrange the sayings to create a kind of "crazy" quilt pattern. Title the bulletin board "Greetings from Around the World."

Bulletin Board Patterns

Wheel of Hats

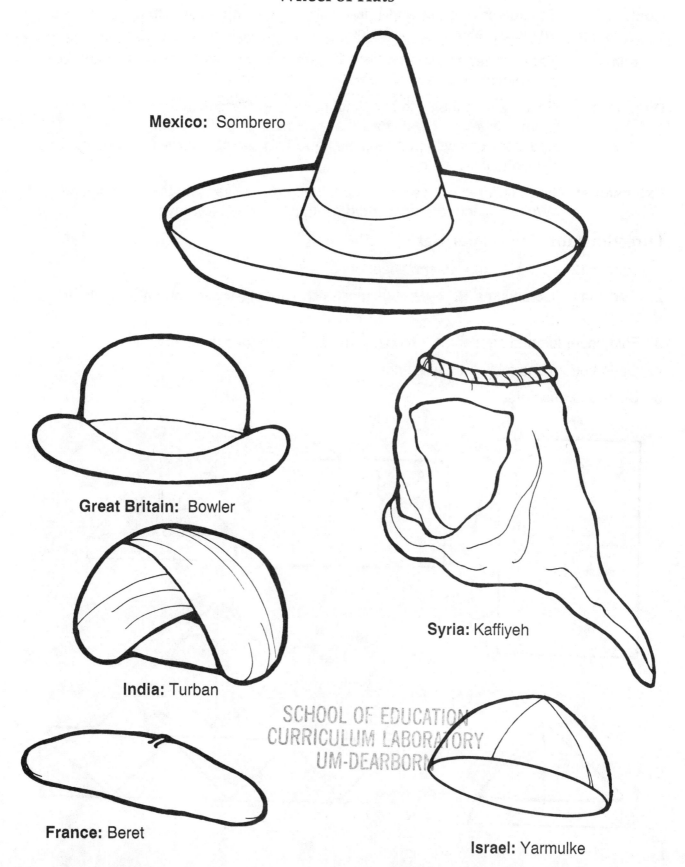

Mexico: Sombrero

Great Britain: Bowler

India: Turban

Syria: Kaffiyeh

France: Beret

Israel: Yarmulke

SCHOOL OF EDUCATION
CURRICULUM LABORATORY
UM-DEARBORN

International Hat Day

Goal: To express ethnicity and individuality by wearing a hat from a child's culture or an individual or original design.

Materials: Paper or newspaper, markers, decorations such as feathers or beads, glue, pipe cleaners, hats from home

Directions: Encourage students to bring in a hat that expresses their ethnicity, or have them design and create hats that express their individuality. Follow the directions below to make simple hats. This can be followed by a hat parade throughout the school.

Extensions: Have children write a story about their hats. Give them the opening line "While running to school one day a gust of wind blew my hat off and..."

Directions for Newspaper Hat

1. Take a 12" x 18" (30 cm x 46 cm) sheet of newspaper.

2. Fold it in half, creating a 12" by 9" (30 cm x 23 cm) sheet—top to bottom with fold at the top.

3. Fold upper left and right corners to join in the middle, then fold in half again.

4. Open bottom and fold up to form brim.

5. Color and decorate.

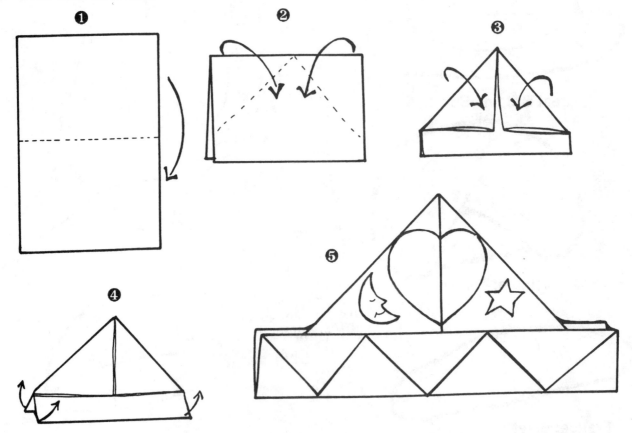

Greetings from Other Countries

Goal: To develop an awareness of how people from other lands greet one another.

Materials: Greetings (see below)

Directions: Have children find and share greetings from their ethnic backgrounds or from a country that interests them. Ask the following questions: "Do you notice similarities in the greeting? " or "Do any of the greetings have accompanying gestures?" Make up a class greeting and a school greeting. Students may work individually or in groups.

Extension: Begin morning announcements with a greeting from another land or have students answer roll call with one of the greetings.

The book, *This is My House,* by Arthur Dorros includes the phrase, "This is my house" in languages from all over the world. By using this book children can learn the phrase.

Greetings From Around the World

France	Bon Jour
Spain	Buenos Días/Hola
Japan	Konichiwa
Polynesia	Aloha
Israel	Shalom
Germany	Guten Tag
Russia	Zdrástvuyte
Sweden	God dag
Czechoslovokia	Dobrý den
Hungary	Jo reggelt
Italy	Buon Giorno
Poland	Dziéndobry
Greece	Kahlee/Maira
Finland	Hyvää päivää

Splatter-Box Greetings

Goal: To say "hello" using a foreign language in an artistic way.

Materials: Shoebox, window screening, old toothbrushes, tempera paint, stapler, staples, paper

Directions:

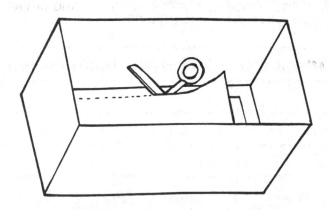

1. Cut the bottom from a shoebox leaving a 1" (2.5 cm) border.

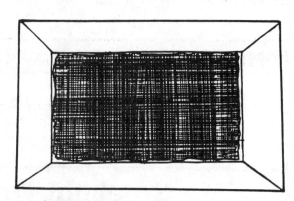

2. Staple window screening securely to inside of the bottom of the box.

3. Cut out a greeting in a foreign language in block or bubble letters. Place the letters on colored paper.

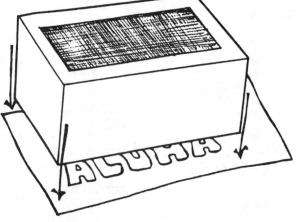

4. Place the box, screen up, over the cut-out letters.

5. Dip old toothbrushes in tempera paint and rapidly brush across the screen to splatter your greeting.

6. Carefully lift off the cut out.

Counting in Foreign Languages

Goal: To experience foreign languages by counting.

Materials: Numbers in different languages (see below).

Directions: Give students the opportunity to count in some languages other than English. Using numbers below, have them pronounce the new words and use them.

Extensions: Make up some simple math problems. Have students solve them and orally give the answers in one of the languages you designate.

Numbers	Italian	Hindi	Spanish	Norwegian
1	uno	ék	uno	en
2	due	do	dos	to
3	tre	teen	tres	tre
4	quattro	chaar	cuatro	fire
5	cinque	paanch	cinco	fem
6	sei	chhe′	seis	seks
7	sette	saat	siete	sju
8	otto	aaTH	ocho	åtte
9	nove	nau	nueve	ni
10	dieci	das	diez	ti

Numbers	Japanese	German	French	Mandarin Chinese
1	ee-CHEE	eins	un	yī
2	nee	zwei	deux	`er
3	sahn	drei	trois	sān
4	shee/yohn	vier	quatre	sz̀
5	goh	fünf	cinq	wǔ
6	roh-KOO	sechs	six	lyòu
7	shee-CHEE	sieben	sept	chì
8	hah-CHEE	acht	huit	bā
9	koo	neun	neuf	jyǒu
10	jōo	zehn	dix	shr′

Community Resources

Goal: To personalize the diversity within your own family and community.

Materials: Guest speakers

Directions: Encourage students to invite parents, grandparents and senior citizens from the community to discuss their family heritage. Speakers are encouraged to bring in pictures, mementoes, and clothing to personalize and share their ethnicity. Discuss the rich multicultural linkage within the class.

Before the speakers come to the class prepare your students. Brainstorm a list of questions that students may wish to ask the speaker. Either keep a list and ask the questions or give each child a copy and have them ask the questions. Some sample questions might be:

1. Where were you born?

2. When did you or your family first come to this country?

3. Why did you come?

4. How is your country different from this country? How is it alike?

5. Are there any special customs, meals, or celebrations from your country?

Have the children write thank-you notes or draw thank-you pictures for the speaker. Encourage them to include some facts they may have learned in listening to the speech. This is a good time to review letter writing with the children.

Extensions: Speakers can be videotaped to share their presentations with other classes.

Ethnic Dress, Fashion, and Adornment

Goal: To know that the variety in fashion and human adornment attests beautifully to the marvelous diversity and ingenuity of people everywhere around the world.

Materials: Books on fashion and period clothes; pictures of people from other lands in their costumes; different articles of clothing, for example: fez, dashiki, kilts, dhoti, etc., paper dolls on page 102

Directions: Reproduce page 102 for children. Let them use the paper doll cut-outs to color, cut, and decorate an ethnic costume similar to one found in their family's heritage or one recently researched.

Extensions: Students share dolls they own and use attached activity sheets.

Encourage children to share pictures or actual items of clothing that represent the diversity within their own classroom. This serves as a way for opening positive discussions about diversity.

Dolls To Dress

Color on clothing that represents your heritage or a country of your choice.

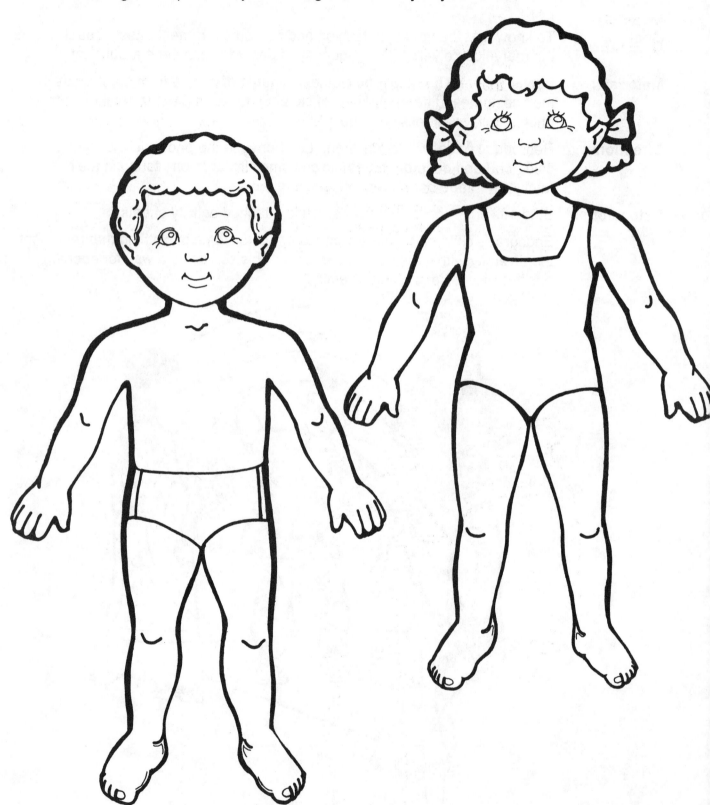

Storytelling

Goal: To develop an awareness of other lands and people through storytelling.

Materials: Stories to tell

Directions: Storytelling is a folk art found in all cultures in the world. Not only is it a great tradition of Native Americans, but the brothers Grimm preserved German stories that had been told for generations; and, in the Middle Ages, troubadours spread heroic and romantic stories throughout the land. Collect several folk stories from around the world (see page 57) that demonstrate what storytelling is all about.

Tell your class a story; don't read it.   Begin by choosing a story you are familiar with or one you would like to become familiar with. Read it aloud or tell it to yourself over and over again until you can really tell it with lots of expression. Use props, gestures, and sound effects. After you have demonstrated, let the children try following the same steps.

Extensions: Have a Storytelling Festival. Have students share their favorite stories with other classes.

My Family Tree

Goal: To research family heritage; to create a family tree as an expression of oneself.

Materials: Pictures, mementoes, family clothing, chart paper, glue, markers, art materials and globe, attached activity sheets

Directions: To illustrate a family tree, children will ask questions of parents, grandparents, aunts, uncles, and others to find out what country or countries are in their family heritage. The children will list their relatives on their picture of a family tree, going back in time as far as possible. They will report on any "famous" relative, or "famous" events participated in by their relatives. The children will further illustrate their family tree or heritage with pictures and mementoes that they have.

Extensions: The teacher may start this unit by sharing his/her family tree.

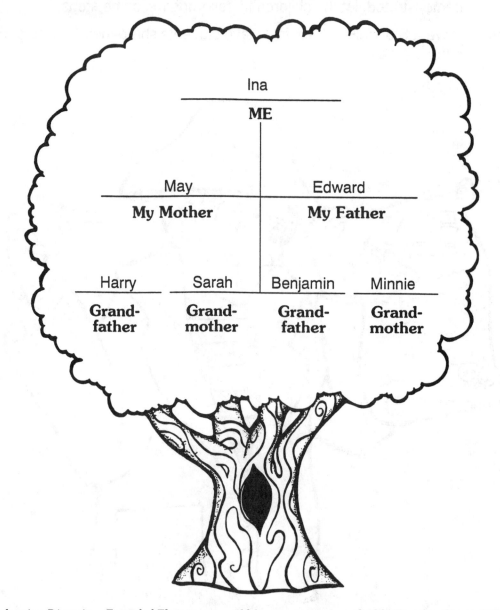

My Family Tree

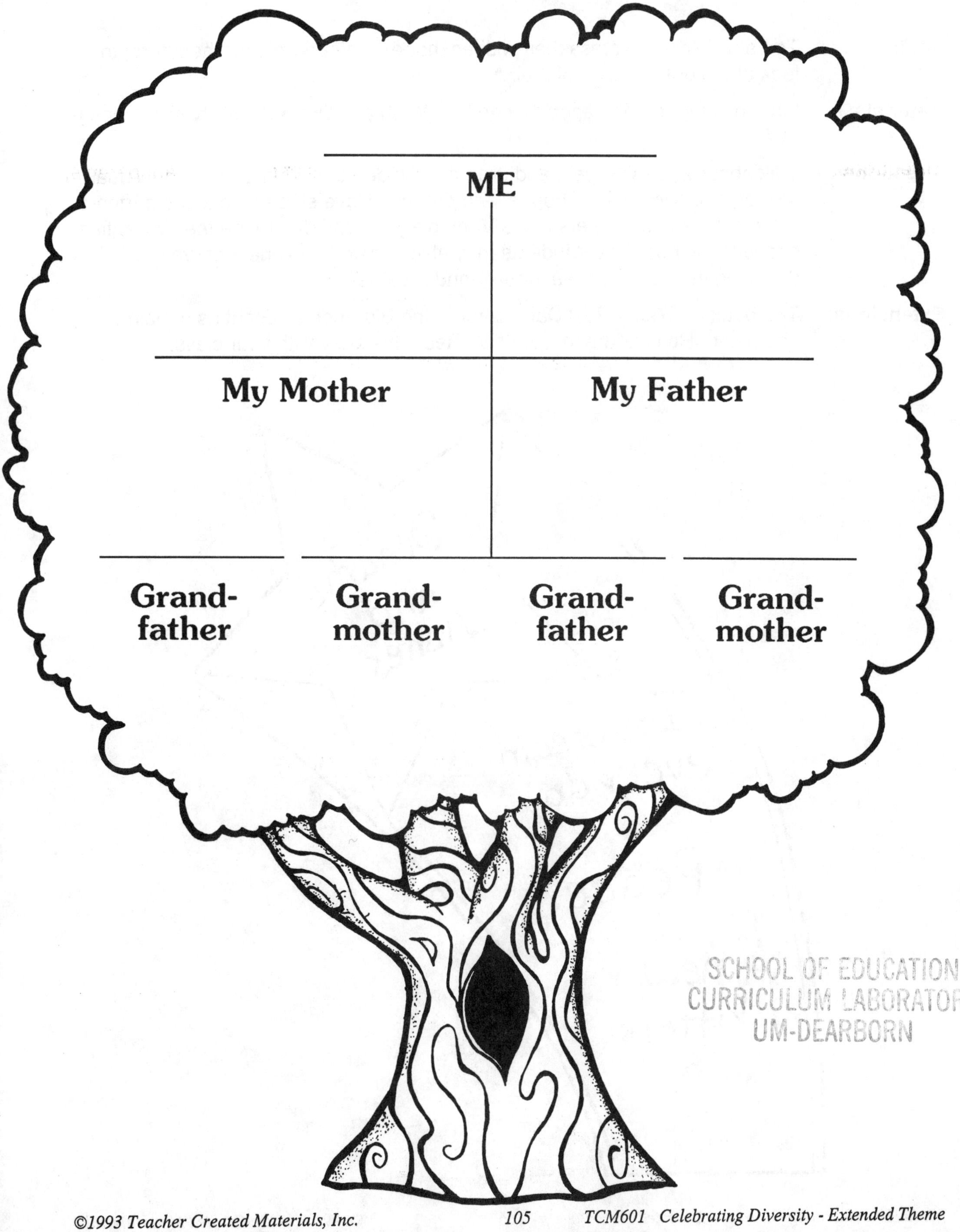

ME

My Mother **My Father**

Grand-father **Grand-mother** **Grand-father** **Grand-mother**

105   *TCM601 Celebrating Diversity - Extended Theme*

SCHOOL OF EDUCATION
CURRICULUM LABORATORY
UM-DEARBORN

Wishes, Hopes, and Dreams

Goal: To help children express their wishes, hopes, and dreams for the future; to look at the positive side of their future.

Materials: large oak tag, graph paper; "When You Wish and Dream" activity sheet (page 107)

Directions: Talk about wishes, hopes, and dreams. Students make their own individual lists of their own wishes, hopes, and dreams. Have students choose partners. Have each set of partners use a Venn diagram and determine the similarities between their choices. Students may also construct a variety of graphs, depicting the class' wishes, hopes, and dreams.

Extensions: The book *B.F.G.* by Roal Dahl features the Big Friendly Giant as a main character. He is a "dream stealer." Read this story with your class.

When You Wish and Dream

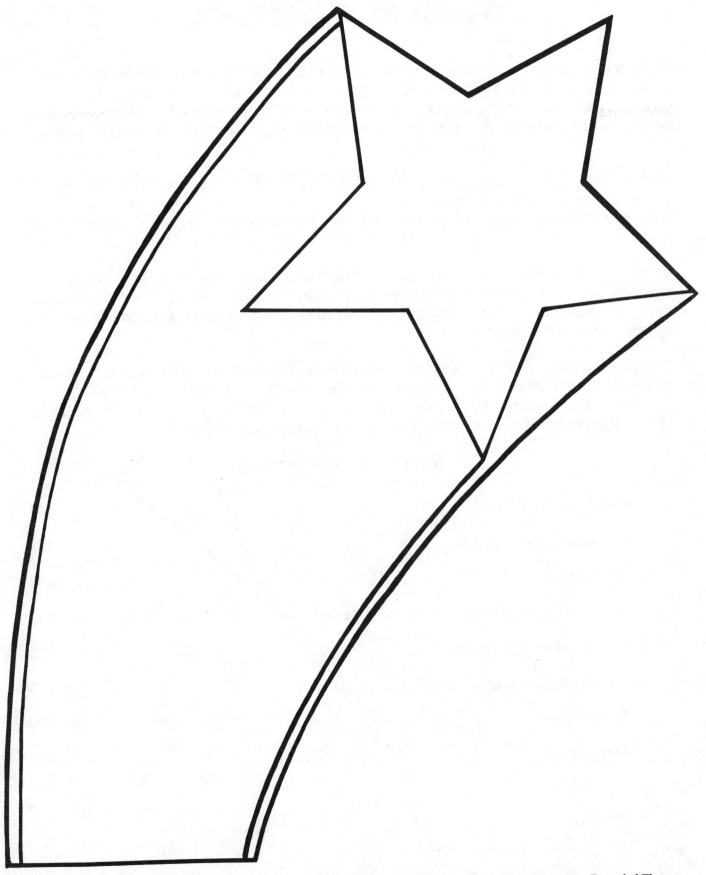

Celebrating International Math and Science

Rockets in space, diseases being treated, and an awareness of the environment, are part of what makes Celebrating International Math and Science such an important unit of the extended theme *Celebrating Diversity.* Let students start by realizing that the earth is really a very small part of a larger group of planets, the solar system. Use the bulletin board on the sun, moon, and earth to emphasize this.

Money and measurement is used throughout the world, but most children are familiar with only what they use on a daily basis. Expand their horizons by measuring items in the classroom both in U.S. customary measure and by playing store using coins from around the world.

Mathematicians and scientists assist us on a daily basis. Their many discoveries help to make our lives safer, healthier, and more enjoyable. Find out more about the individuals who have contributed so much to our lives by reading some books and sharing some of their biographies with the children.

Incorporate math and science wherever you see it. As the students line up outside the room on the playground talk about the length and shape of the lines, or count off and see if they understand about adding one. Whatever you choose to do, explain that the same concepts are used throughout the world, making math and science an international study.

Mini Table of Contents

Bulletin Board Ideas

Sun, Moon, and Earth

Set up a bulletin board. Back it with light blue construction paper or fabric. Title it, "There Is Just One Moon and One Golden Sun." Subtitle it, "It's a Small World." Make large construction paper circles to represent the moon, the sun, and the earth. Make the moon white, the earth dark blue, and the sun yellow. Place them on the bulletin board according to the picture below. Put three envelopes across the bottom of the bulletin board. On one write "Earth Facts," on another "Moon Facts," and on the other "Sun Facts." Copy or cut out the facts on page 110 and glue them onto index cards. Place them into the proper envelope. Each day have a student select one fact and share it with the class. Pin it near the appropriate heavenly body.

Bulletin Board Ideas *(cont.)*

Sun Facts

About 1,300,000 planets the size of earth would fit into the sun.
The sun is really a star.
The sun is about 93 million miles (150 million kilometers) from the earth.
Light from the sun reaches the earth in about 8 minutes and 20 seconds.
The sun is a ball of gas that has a temperature at the center of about 27 million degrees Fahrenheit (15 million degrees Celsius).
Sunlight travels at 186,282 miles (298,051 kilometers) per second.

Earth Facts

Half of the earth is always covered with sunlight.
The earth is always turning.
When you are getting ready for bed, on the other side of the earth children are just getting up.
The earth is one of nine planets that moves around the sun.
The center of the earth is about 4,000 miles (6400 kilometers) under your feet.
The earth's nearest neighbor is the moon.

Moon Facts

There is no air or water on the moon. It is made of gray rock, some of it covered with dust.
The moon is about 239,000 miles (382,000 kilometers) away from the earth.
The moon is like a giant mirror. The light it sends to the earth is light reflected from the sun.
As the moon revolves around the earth, it seems to change shapes. These are called the phases of the moon.
American astronauts walked on the moon in 1969.
Most craters on the moon are five to ten miles (8 to 16 kilometers) wide.
You could jump six times higher on the moon than earth because its gravity isn't as strong as the earth's.

It's In the Stars

Goal: To learn about constellations seen the world over.

Materials: Constellation chart (page 112), paper, pencils

Directions: Talk about the fact that everyone lives on the same planet. Ask children that if we all live on the same planet then when we look up in the sky shouldn't we all see the same thing? Their immediate response will probably be yes. If it's nighttime ask what they would see. Their answers should include the moon and stars. Then explain that they also see constellations. Constellations are stars that we join together with imaginary lines to represent pictures. These "pictures" have been named after what they resemble. They have often been used to help travelers find their directions. The names of the constellations are in Latin. Some of the constellations include Draco (Dragon), Ursa Major (Great Bear), Ursa Minor (Little Bear), and Cygnus (Swan).

However when children who live in the Northern Hemisphere look up, they will see different constellations, than if they live in the Southern Hemisphere. People living in the southern United States, Hawaii, or northern Australia sometimes get to see constellations from both hemispheres.

Determine in which hemisphere you live; then reproduce the constellations that are appropriate to your hemisphere. On a clear starry night have the children go out with a parent and look up into the sky. What constellations can they see? Have them write them down and draw them. Have them make circles for the stars and connect them.

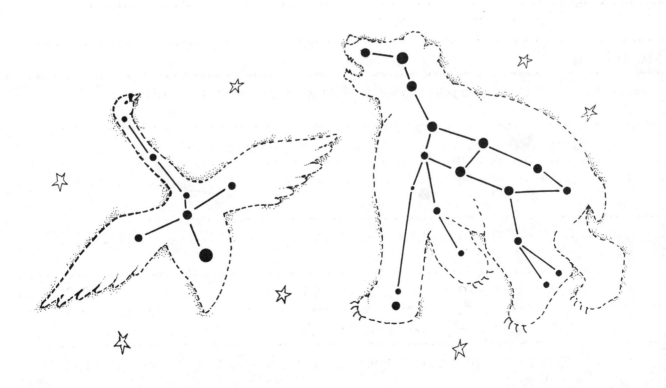

Constellation Chart

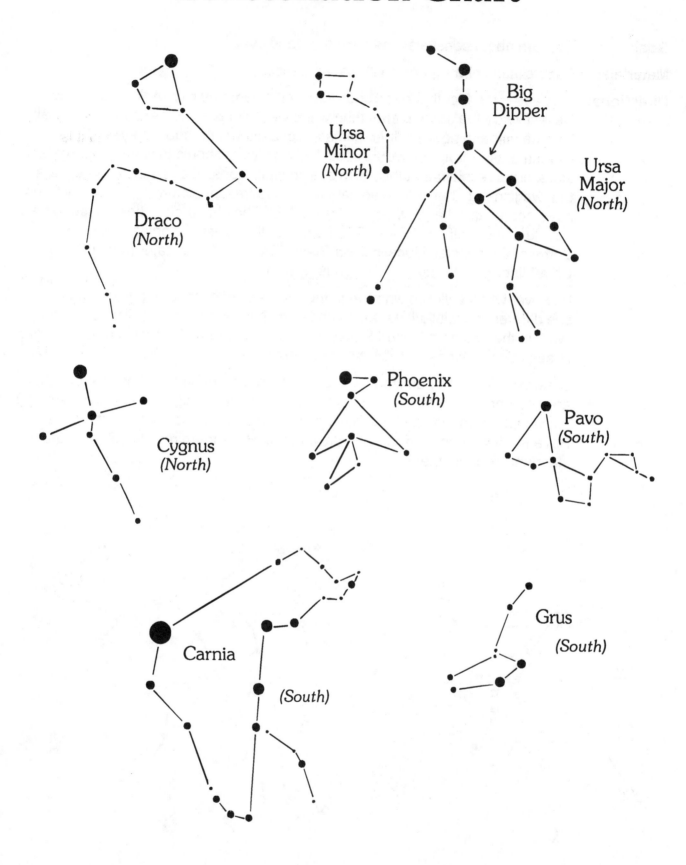

The Abacus

Goal: To create and experience the use of an abacus.

Materials: Plastic foam meat tray, 4 thin bamboo skewers, 21 colored cereal O's (3 different colors, 7 O's of each color), tape, craft knife (optional)

Directions: Explain that an abacus is an ancient mathematical device. Ancient Romans and Greeks used the abacus. It is still used throughout the world. In China it is called a suanpan which means "counting board." An abacus can be used to perform many mathematical operations such as adding, subtracting, multiplying, and dividing.

To make an abacus use the materials listed above and do the following:

1. Cut out the center section of a meat tray with scissors or craft knife.

2. Place seven O's of the same color on one skewer. Repeat with remaining two colors and skewers. Tape skewers vertically to the back of the cut meat tray.

3. Add the fourth bamboo skewer horizontally on the back of the meat tray, dividing the O's two above and five below the skewer.

The abacus is now ready to use.

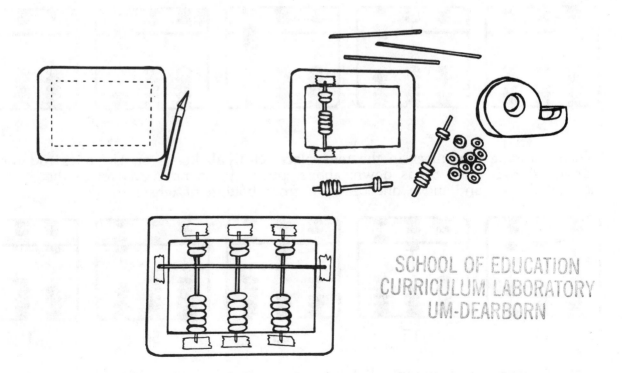

SCHOOL OF EDUCATION
CURRICULUM LABORATORY
UM-DEARBORN

How To Use the Abacus

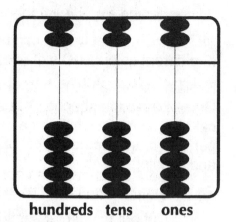

hundreds tens ones

Only beads (O's) touching the horizontal rod are being counted. Each rod has a place value

When representing the numbers 1-9, use the ones rod; 10-99, tens and ones rods; 100-199, hundreds, tens, and ones rods.

Here are some ones place examples:

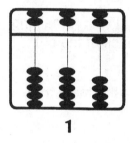 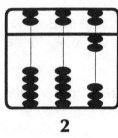 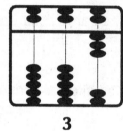 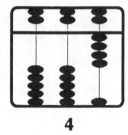

1   **2**   **3**   **4**

When showing a number value of five or more, move the four bottom beads back down away from horizontal rod and bring down one bead from above horizontal rod (which represents 5) and any other necessary beads:

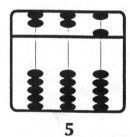 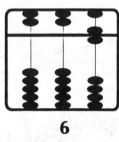 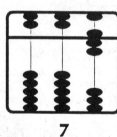 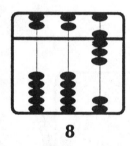 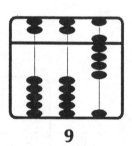

5   **6**   **7**   **8**   **9**

When showing a number in the tens place, clear all beads on the ones rod (below horizontal rod, push beads down; above, push up, so no beads touch the horizontal rod) and move one bead up from bottom of tens rod:

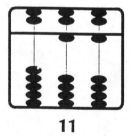 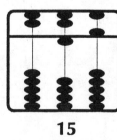 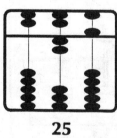 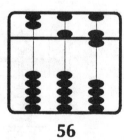 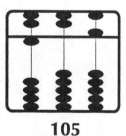

11   **15**   **25**   **56**   **105**

Have students try counting 1-100 (or higher) or calculate simple addition and subtraction problems!

Biographies of Famous Scientists and Mathematicians

Goal:　　To learn about a person who has made major discoveries and contributions to society; to realize that every culture has its share of creative, talented people.

Materials:　Ethnic newspapers, magazines, books, journals, history books, report form (page 116)

Directions:　With the class, brainstorm a list of famous scientists and mathematicians from around the world. With younger children choose some books about some of these people and read them. Have older children do some research on their own. Let them use the forms on page 116 to formalize their learning.

Extensions:　Locate a list of Nobel Prize winners. (An encyclopedia is one source.) Explain that Alfred Nobel invented dynamite—for something other than death and destruction. He established a fund with 9 million dollars which was designed to acknowledge great men and women of achievement the world over. Find out which categories and which countries are represented by the Nobel Prize.

Biography of a Famous Mathematician or Scientist

Directions: Choose the proper form to complete a report about a famous mathematician or scientist from anywhere in the world.

Famous Mathematician

Name: _____

Country of birth: _____

Date of birth: _____

Famous for: _____

Prizes won: _____

This mathematician has made life better because _____

_____

_____

_____

_____

Famous Scientist

Name: _____

Country of birth: _____

Date of birth: _____

Famous for: _____

Prizes won: _____

This scientist has made life better because _____

_____

_____

_____

_____

Animals of the Rain Forest

Goal: To develop awareness of some of the many creatures that live in the rain forest.

Materials: Magazines such as *National Geographic* and *Ranger Rick*, picture books about the rain forest, encyclopedias

Directions: Talk about animals of the rain forest with your class. Explain that many are in danger of losing their homes unless people all over the world become more aware of taking care of rain forests. As a class, create a background that shows the layers of the rain forest which include a top layer, canopy, understory, and floor. These can be represented by using different colors of construction paper for each and having children draw in trees.

Have each student choose an animal found in the rain forest. A list is provided below. Each child draws his or her animal. Cut around the animal and place it on the rain forest background.

Extensions: Students make "Save the Rain Forest" posters.

- emerald tree boa
- spider monkey
- morpho butterfly
- tarantula
- arrow-poison frog
- three-toed sloth
- hawk
- tapir
- orangutan
- jaguar
- toucan
- boa constrictor
- bee
- anteaters
- porcupines

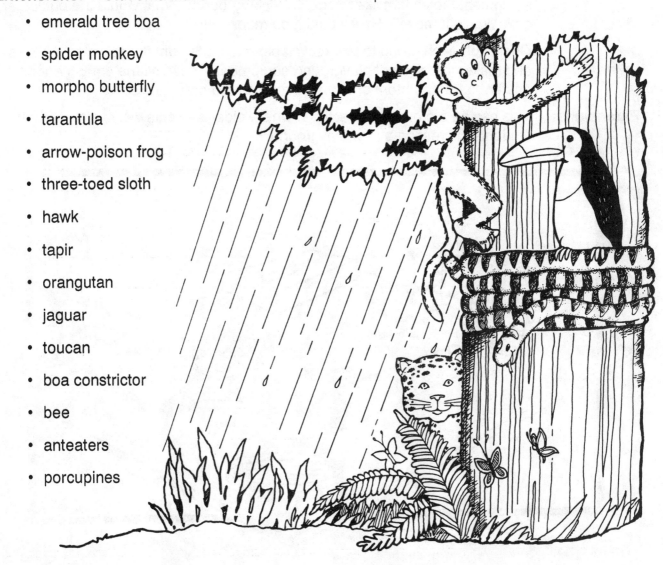

Building a "Recyclable" Playground

Goal: To make children aware of recycling as a way to protect the earth; to create a model playground using recyclable materials.

Materials: Variety of recyclable materials, large cardboard cartons, glue, scissors, tape, large cardboard box or poster board, recycling worksheet (page 119), green paint, paintbrush

Directions: Before beginning the project, talk about recyclable materials. Set up a recycling center in your class. Explain that recycling is an important thing to do if one considers that every day so many styrofoam cups are used they could circle the globe. This can be accomplished with boxes that are labeled "Recyclable." Use the worksheet on page 119 to make children more aware of recycling.

Discuss with children that all over the world children play in playgrounds. Let the children talk about their favorite playgrounds and what type of play equipment is found there. Then, in small groups, have them brainstorm equipment they might like to see on a playground. What would the equipment do? Would it move? How would it be made safe?

Challenge each group to use recyclable materials from the recyclable boxes and make one piece of playground equipment. Place all the equipment on a poster board or bottom of a box carton painted green. Display.

Extensions: This can be a cross-grade activity, where older students work with younger students in creating a new playground.

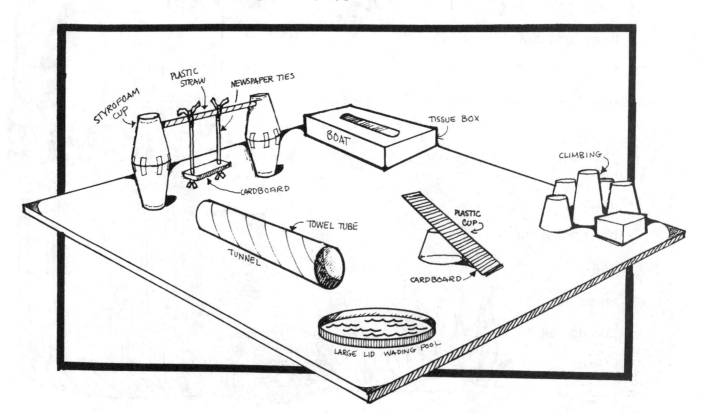

Recycling Worksheet

List items you can recycle

_____

_____

_____

_____

_____

_____

_____

List the items you can't recycle

_____

_____

_____

_____

_____

_____

_____

_____

_____

School Store

Goal: To teach children that money is used all over the world.

Materials: Various sizes of boxes, empty product boxes, cash box, tables, real coins from around the world or reproduced from page 121, price tags

Directions: Set up a model store. Make several sets of price tags for products you will sell. (Sticky notes work well for this.) Have each tag display a different currency.

Show the children the currency that different countries have. Tell them what each coin is called. If you are using real coins let them feel the money. Make comparisons to money of about the same value to your currency.

Decide on which currency to use, and make a set of price tags. Put them on the products and let the children play store. They should practice playing the roles of customers and store employees so they all have the opportunity of being both buyer and seller.

Change the price tags for each type of currency you use.

Coins From Around the World

Australia

Bahamas

Austria

Canada

Denmark

England

Switzerland

Singapore

Italy

New Zealand

India

Mexico

China

Belgium

Germany

Measurement

Goal: To experience a few forms of measurement.

Materials: Standard and metric rulers

Directions: Explain that there is more than one form of measurement. Students are going to have the opportunity to use both customary measure using inches, and metric measure using centimeters. Give students both standard and metric rulers or reproduce the ruler below for each to use.

Choose two or three locations in your classroom or school. The children should measure in inches or centimeters using the rulers. Then have them convert or remeasure using the other form of measure.

Extension: Set up a class chart that shows the areas that are measured using both types of measurement.

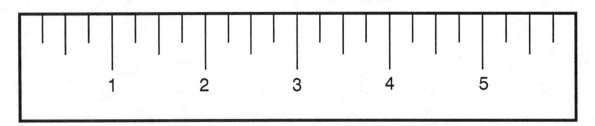

Inches

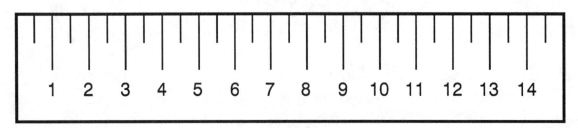

Centimeters

Celebrating International Food and Cooking

Food! What other word conjures up the use of so many senses? What else but food gives us the smell of bread baking in the oven, the sight of a green salad being tossed, the sound of popcorn hitting the top of a pot, the velvety-smooth sweet taste of ice cream as we lick a cone, or the feel of a prickly pineapple skin. And what else but food has for all ages brought people together to bake bread.

As you celebrate international food and cooking, let children share their favorite types of foods. Choose a food that is eaten around the world such as bread or rice and find out how it is presented differently in each country.

How is food cooked? Is bread always baked in an oven? Are pancakes only made in a frying pan? Is pizza always cooked on a pan? Find out some of these answers and then try some of these ways of cooking in your classroom.

What foods are part of celebrations? Is a wedding or birthday ever complete without a cake? What foods do children associate with holidays? Do they eat the same foods as others in the class or others around the world on those special days? Ask these questions and more as you celebrate international food and cooking.

Mini Table of Contents

Bulletin Board Ideas

Look What's Cooking

Collect menus and place mats from ethnic restaurants. Ask students to contribute these items. Use the place mats as a background for the bulletin board. Reproduce and enlarge the fork, knife, spoon, and, napkin pattern on page 125. Put them on the bulletin board to form a table setting. Use the space where a plate would be for changing display during this unit.

In this spot hang menus that students have brought in from ethnic restaurants.

Add photographs taken of students as they cook in class. Feature charts and recipes.

Bulletin Board Patterns

A Family Cookbook

Goal: To share and explore foods common to students' ethnic heritage or a country of interest.

Materials: Recipes from home, recipe cards

Directions: Reproduce the recipe card on page 127 for students to take home. Students bring in recipes that express their ethnicity or recipes from a country of their own choosing. Recipes are collected and put together in a class cookbook. Have them share with the class any experiences they may have had with the recipe. These can later be used in a school cookbook. Create a cookbook cover. Let students take part in designing this. Allow students to check out the class cookbook.

Extensions: These recipes can be the basis for a school-wide cookbook.

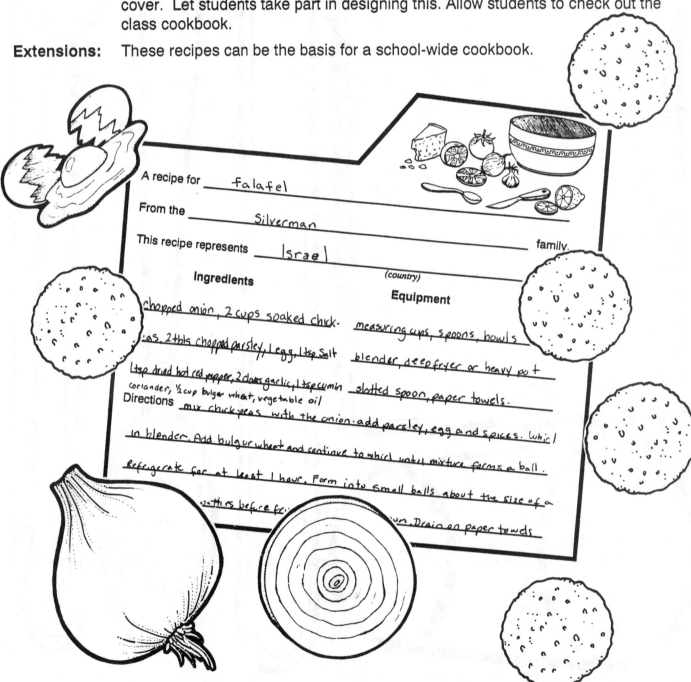

A recipe for _____falafel_____

From the _____Silverman_____

This recipe represents _____Israel_____ family.
(country)

Ingredients

Equipment

chopped onion, 2 cups soaked chick-
:as. 2 tbls chopped parsley, 1 egg, 1 tsp salt
1 tsp dried hot red pepper, 2 cloves garlic, 1 tsp cumin
coriander, ½ cup bulgar wheat, vegetable oil

measuring cups, spoons, bowls
blender, deep fryer or heavy pot
slotted spoon, paper towels.

Directions mix chickpeas with the onion. add parsley, egg and spices. Whirl
in blender. Add bulgur wheat and continue to whirl until mixture forms a ball.
Refrigerate for at least 1 hour. Form into small balls about the size of a
...this before fr: ...un. Drain on paper towels

Recipe Card

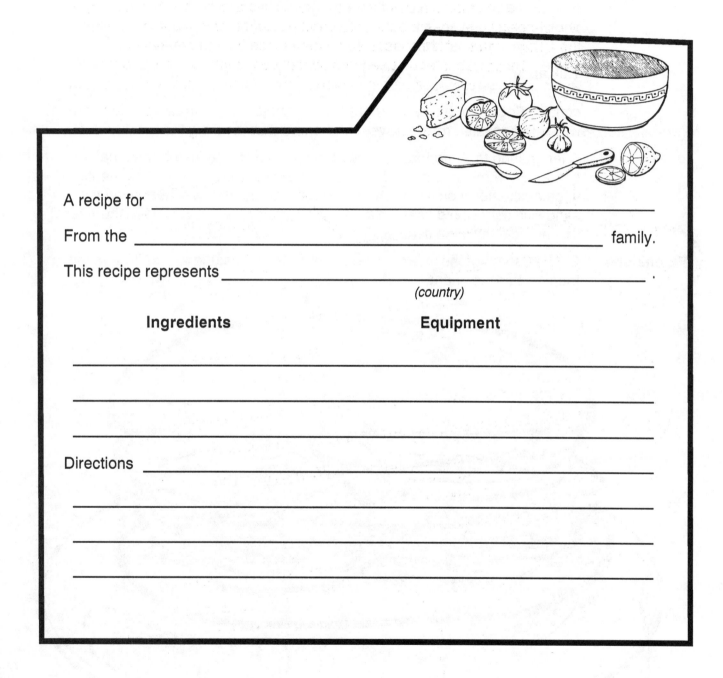

A recipe for _____

From the _____ family.

This recipe represents _____ .
(country)

Ingredients	Equipment

_____

_____

_____

Directions _____

_____

_____

_____

_____

An International Sandwich

Goal: To create an international sandwich.

Materials: Worksheet, page 129, pencils, crayons

Directions: Begin by asking children if anyone has eaten a sandwich for lunch. Have children take turns describing their sandwiches. Draw comparisons and contrasts among the different sandwiches. Ask some of the following questions: Did everyone have the same type of bread? What were some of the fillings in the sandwiches? How many of them were meat?

Talk about how the sandwich was born. Sandwich Day originated on October 14, 1744. The story goes that the Earl of Sandwich, an eighteenth century English nobleman, ordered a servant to bring him two slices of bread with some roasted meat between the bread thus creating the first sandwich.

After sharing this information, have the children create an international sandwich. First have them decide what type of bread, filling, condiments, or vegetables they would use. After they have decided, have them draw the sandwich they would assemble onto the plate on page 129. Have them label the ingredients in the sandwich.

Extensions: Choose some of the international sandwiches that students create and make them in class to share.

An International Sandwich *(cont.)*

Draw your international sandwich on this plate.

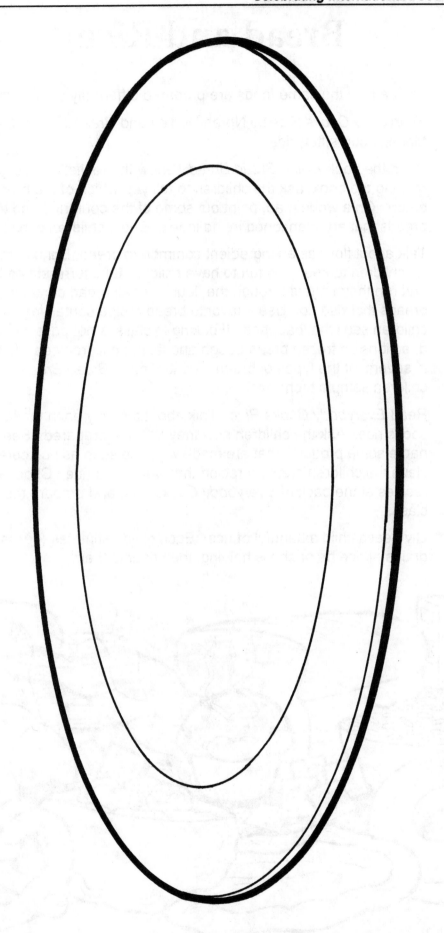

Bread and Rice

Goal: To see how the same foods are prepared differently all over the world.

Materials: *Everybody Cooks Rice* by Norah Dooley and *Bread Bread Bread* by Ann Morris, flour, sifter, rice

Directions: Read the book *Bread Bread Bread*. Show the realistic photographs. After reading the book, ask the children to tell you which of the breads they have eaten. On a world map, point out some of the countries and the type of breads that are mentioned in the index. See if children can remember these.

Talk about flour as an ingredient common to bread. Bring some kind of flour in for children to see. It is fun to have children take turns sifting flour onto paper and run their fingers through the flour. Not all bread contains yeast, but most breads that rise do. Use a favorite bread recipe containing yeast and let children see what happens. If baking in class is not possible follow the directions on frozen bread dough and let the children see what happens. Bring in several of the types of breads mentioned in *Bread Bread Bread* and let the children sample them.

Read *Everybody Cooks Rice.* Talk about the way each family in the book cooks rice. Ask the children how they like rice prepared. See if they can name some products that are made with rice such as rice cereal or rice cakes. Have the children create a recipe that would use rice. Choose some of the recipes at the back of *Everybody Cooks Rice* and prepare them with your class.

Extension: Give each child a handful of rice. Each child estimates (guesses) how many grains of rice he or she is holding, then counts them.

Spices Around the World

Goal: To become familiar with spices used in cooking around the world.

Materials: A variety of spices, baby food jars or small containers with lids, a nail, hammer, masking tape, marker

Directions: Before beginning this lesson, put a small amount of different spices into several different jars. Poke holes in the lids and put them on the jars. Write the name of the spice and the country of origin on a strip of masking tape. Some common spices and where they are grown are listed below.

Cardamom — Malalbar, India, Jamaica

Caraway — Europe, Asia, northern United States

Clove — Indonesia, West Indies, Madagascar, Tanzania

Ginger — Asia, Japan, West Indies, South America, western Africa

Paprika — Tropical America

Vanilla — South America

Nutmeg — Spice Islands

Explain that spices come from different parts of plants including the bark of the tree such as cinnamon, the fruit of a plant such as pepper, the buds such as cloves, or roots such as ginger. It is spices that give foods different flavors. Food without any spices can often seem bland.

Spices are generally very aromatic. Give children a chance to smell spices by passing around the jars. Let them guess what spices they might be smelling. Ask how it smells. Make a class graph of their favorite and least favorite spices.

Culminating Activities

A culminating activity is an exciting way to conclude your extended theme on *Celebrating Diversity*. It allows students a chance to synthesize their learning to produce a product or engage in an activity that can be shared with others. What better way to culminate this unit than to have an international celebration. In the pages that follow you will find information that can be used to create a major celebration. You may opt to do only one of the activities that follow, or you may want to complete them all. They can be adapted to include other classes of the same grade level, a "buddy" class, the entire school, parents, and the community.

Mini Table of Contents

An International Festival

Goal: To foster an awareness of foods from around the world, to foster cooperative learning and to celebrate the year's end.

Materials: Foods prepared by students and their parents, cookbooks, menus, place mats.

Directions: Plan an international dinner with your students and their parents. Use the invitation on page 134.

Enlist parents to help in the planning, preparing and serving of the food. Let children help decorate using an international theme through flags or representative decorations and colors. They can make place mats and place cards for each family member who will be attending. Foods can be served while you display the country's flag. Provide a copy of the recipe to share with all. The recipe "alerts" those with food allergies.

Plan a program for the evening. Greet your guests in several different languages. Provide a combination of activities. Choose to have some "Morning Sharing" (page 135) or "Walk the Halls" (page 137). Play some games such as "Limbo" or "Klassa." Share a biography of a famous international mathematician or scientist.

Present awards for a job well done. (page 140)

Extensions: Combine several classes to have an international dinner day. Provide entertainment such as games or music. (See the music and movement section.)

Please join us for a celebration!

Time: _____

Place: _____

Location: _____

Date: _____

Would you please bring _____

_____

_____

_____

_____

We look forward to you joining us.

Morning Sharing

Goal: To develop an awareness of our rich cultural diversity through story, music, and song; to strengthen oral language and listening skills.

Materials: Stories, books, or poems from around the world; individual student readers

Directions: Each morning a student or class may choose to share a favorite song, story, or poem. Children may read or tell their stories. Children can tape stories which can be placed at a listening center for use by other students.

Extensions: Let children share their favorites with the entire school. If there is a loud speaker system, let a few children read or recite each day.

Celebration of World Holidays

Goal: To foster an awareness of a variety of holidays celebrated around the world.

Materials: See individual activities.

Directions: As there are so many holidays celebrated around the world, a worthwhile activity is to find out about and then recreate how some of these holidays are celebrated. A brief description of a few holidays and a suggested activity for each is given. Other activities to include are signs, songs, games, stories, pictures, ceremonies, and foods.

New Year's Day — In Japan, bells ring 108 times to rid evil on January Ist. Every child celebrates a new birthday and wears a new kimono. Families decorate houses with rice cakes and sweet-smelling pine. They pay off their debts. In the United States, there are parties, parades, and football games. In Greece, a New Year's cake called a *peta* is baked with a coin inside to bring good luck, while in Hungary, a pig roasted with a four-leaf clover is supposed to bring good luck. In Sweden, people attend church and have a big family dinner.

Activity: Create symbols that might represent good luck such as horseshoes or four-leaf clovers.

April Fool's Day — Celebrated throughout the world, the first day of April is a day that people play tricks on each other. In England, the tricks are played only until noon, in Scotland, people are sent on foolish errands, while in France, the person fooled is called a Poisson d'Avril or an April fish. People in France buy chocolate fish in honor of the day. The holiday is said to have started over 400 years ago in France when New Year's Day was held on March 25 and celebrated through April 1. When a new calendar was adopted, people forgot about the change in dates and tricks were played on them by those who remembered the change.

Activity: Make paper fish to represent the chocolate ones. Use brown paper and have children decorate them.

Octoberfest — This October festival was first held in 1810 in Germany as a celebration of the wedding of King Ludwig and his queen, Theresa. Today it is a time for eating, drinking, and having a good time. There are parades, floats, shows, and picnics.

Activity: Have an Octoberfest feast in your classroom. Try different types of foods such as sausages and cheeses. Afterward have a classroom parade.

Boxing Day — This is a national holiday in England, Australia, and New Zealand. It is celebrated the day after Christmas, December 26th. It comes from either the custom of opening the church poor boxes the day after Christmas or from boys who were learning trades visiting their master's customers with boxes to collect gifts.

Activity: Have children create a special box and decorate it.

Walk the Halls

Goal: To highlight an awareness of the year's activities and to view the diversity within your school.

Materials: Decorated classrooms or hallways

Directions: Invite classes to walk through your classroom and view the year's displays. Key features should be the quilts, flags, and the international art gallery. Hallways that are decorated with student materials would be ideal. Inviting parents and the community in to see the displays would be an added touch for the students. Allow them to act as tour guides or docents explaining the projects they have completed.

Extensions: Have as many classes as possible participate. If there is more than one classroom involved in *Celebrating Diversity* include them on the tour. This might be coordinated as an all-school event.

Totem Pole

Goal: To provide an opportunity for children from all grades to work together.

Materials: Clean, round ice cream cartons, glue, paint, paintbrushes, tape, construction paper, recycled materials

Directions: Show pictures of totem poles. Let students see that they are three-dimensional. Explain that a totem is a symbol for a tribe, clan, or family. A totem pole is a carving of animals, birds, fish, plants, or other natural objects that would represent a Native American tribe. After looking at some pictures, let children decide what they would like their totem pole to represent. Let them design on paper a model of what they want to build.

Stack the cartons one on top of another to a desired height. Tape them together and cover with construction paper. Tape or glue on recycled materials such as paper cups or newspaper strips to form faces or designs. Paint when dry. Use acrylic paint or tempera paint.

Extensions: Younger children may work with older children to create a totem pole.

World Flag Quilt

Goal: To foster cooperative work; to provide closure to the theme.

Materials: A collection of scraps of material in all colors, needles, thread, glue, and pictures of flags

Directions: The students create flags of the world from the cloth which has been collected. They will work as a class or on individual projects. The idea of pairing younger children with older children would work well here. As the flags are completed, they should be sewn together to form a quilt. Parent volunteers would work well to help with the sewing. The quilt may be used as a wall hanging.

Extensions: If a sewing project is not possible, substitute with construction paper, glue, and butcher paper. Have children complete quilt pieces made from butcher paper. Use construction paper strips to finish off the quilt.

A school-wide project can be made if several classes complete quilt squares and they are assembled into a large quilt.

Awards

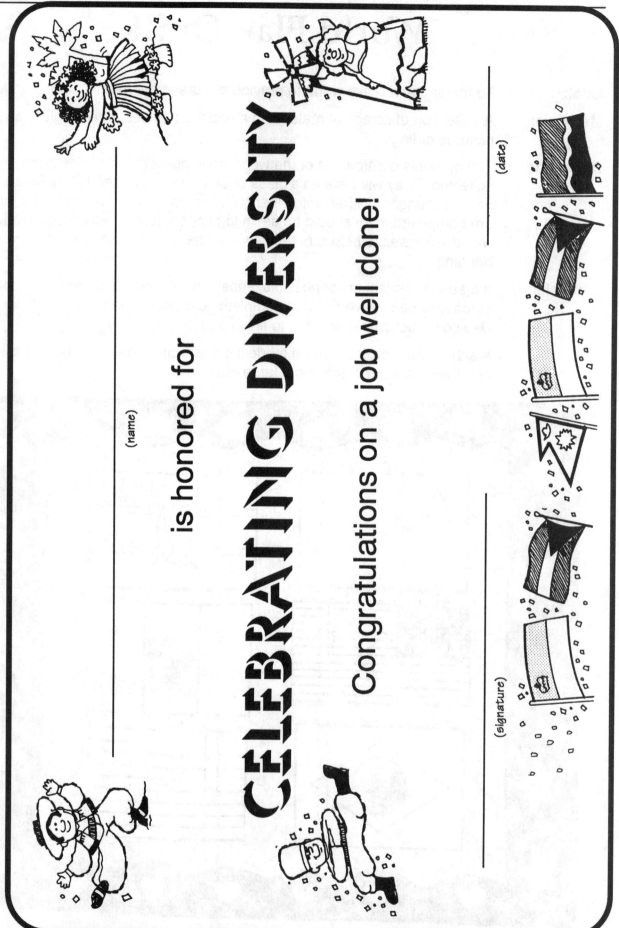

_____
(name)

is honored for

CELEBRATING DIVERSITY

Congratulations on a job well done!

_____
(date)

_____
(signature)

Awards *(cont.)*

Give these "great job" tickets to students as you find them doing a great job.

Give these bookmarks to students as they read books celebrating diversity.

World Map

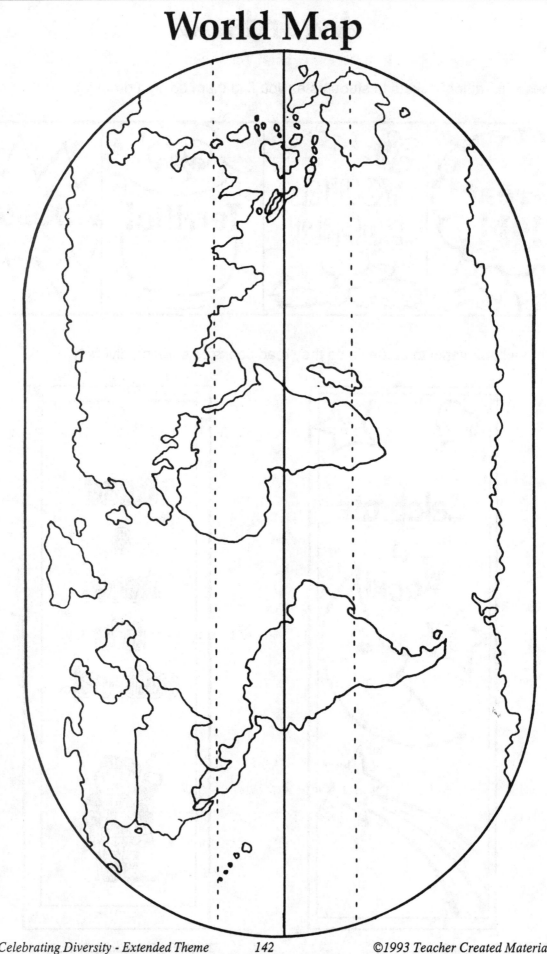

Bibliography

Aardema, Verna. *Borreguita and the Coyote: A Tale from Ayulta, Mexico.* Knopf, 1991

Baer, Edith. *This Is the Way We Go to School.* Scholastic, 1990

Brusca, Maria Cristiana. *On the Pampas.* Henry Holt, 1991

Buhler, Cheryl, Nolan N. Fossum, and Paula Spence, annotated by. *An Annotated Bibliography of Thematic Literature.* Teacher Created Materials, 1993

Bunting, Eve. *Fly Away Home.* Clarion, 1991

Bunting, Eve. *The Wall.* Houghton Mifflin, 1990

Carlstrom, Nancy White. *Baby-O.* Little, Brown, 1992

Cherry, Lynne. *The Great Kapok Tree.* HBJ, 1990

Dooley, Norah. *Everybody Cooks Rice.* Carolrhoda Books, 1991

Dorros, Arthur. *Abuela.* Dutton, 1991

Dorros, Arthur. *This Is My House.* Scholastic, 1992

Dorros, Arthur. *Tonight Is Carnaval.* Dutton, 1991

Downing, Julie. *Mozart Tonight.* Macmillan, 1991

The Earth Works Group. *50 Simple Things Kids Can Do To Save the Earth.* Andrews and McMeel, 1990

Faber, Doris. *The Amish.* Chelsea House, 1986

Goble, Paul. *Buffalo Woman.* Macmillan, 1987

Greenfield, Eloise. *Africa Dream.* Harper Collins, 1989

Gutierrez, Douglas. *The Night of the Stars.* Kane-Miller, 1988

Haskins, Jim. *Count Your Way Through the Arab World.* (China, Japan, Mexico). Carolrhoda Books, 1987-1991

Heide, Florence Parry and Judith Heide Gilliland. *The Day of Ahmed's Secret.* Lothrop, Lee, & Shephard, 1990

Heine, Helme. *Prince Bear.* Macmillan, 1989

Ho, Minfong. *The Clay Marble.* Farrar, Straus, & Giroux, 1991

Howard, Elizabeth. *Aunt Flossie's Hats (And Crab Cakes Later).* Houghton Mifflin, 1991

Hudson, Wade. *Jamal's Busy Day.* Just Us Books, 1991

Jeffers, Susan. *Brother Eagle, Sister Sky: A Message from Chief Seattle.* Dial Books, 1991

Joesph, Lynn. *Coconut Kind of Day: Island Poems.* Puffin Books, 1992

Joosse, Barbara. *Mama Do You Love Me?* Chronicle Books, 1991

Keegan, Marsha. *Pueblo Boy: Growing Up in Two Worlds.* Dutton, 1991

Bibliography *(cont.)*

Kendall, Russ. *Eskimo Boy: Life in an Inupiag Eskimo Village.* Scholastic, 1992

Ker Wilson, Barbara. *The Turtle and the Island.* B. Lippincott, 1990

Kipling, Rudyard. *Just So Stories.* Harper Collins, 1991

Kollar, Judith, annotated by. *Multicultural Bibliography.* Teacher Created Materials, 1993

Lehtinen, Ritva and Kair E. Nurmi. *The Grandchildren of the Incas.* Carolrhoda Books, 1991

Lewis, Richard. *All of You Was Singing.* Macmillan, 1991

Lindstroms, Eva. *The Cat Hat.* Kane-Miller Books, 1989

Mills, Lauren. *The Rag Coat.* Little, 1991

Milnes, Gerald. *Granny Will Your Dog Bite? and Other Mountain Rhymes.* Knopf, 1990

Osborne, Mary Pope. *American Tall Tales.* Knopf, 1976

Say, Allen. *Tree of Cranes.* Houghton Mifflin, 1991

Shannon, George. *More Stories to Solve.* Greenwillow, 1991

Steptoe, John. *Mufaro's Beautiful Daughters.* Scholastic, 1987

Strickland, Dorthy. *Listen Children.* Bantam, 1986

Surat, Michele Maria. *Angel Child, Dragon Child.* Scholastic, 1983

Swartz, Howard and Barbara Rush. *The Diamond Tree: Jewish Tales From Around the World.* Harper Collins, 1991

van Straalen, Alice. *The Book of Holidays Around the World.* E.P. Dutton, 1986

Wahl, Jan. *Tailypo!* Henry Holt & Co., 1991

Waters, Kate. *Lion Dancer.* Scholastic, 1990

Wettasinghe, Sybal. *The Umbrella Thief.* Kane-Miller Books, 1987

Winter, Geanette. *Diego.* Knopf, 1991

Winthrop, Elizabeth. *Vasilissa The Beautiful: A Russian Folk Tale.* Harper Collins, 1991

Wolkstein, Diane. *The Banza.* Dial Books Young, 1981

Yep, Laurence. *Child of the Owl.* Harper Collins, 1990

Yep, Laurence. *Dragonwings.* Harper Collins, 1977

Zhensun, Zheng and Alice Low. *A Young Painter: The Life and Paintings of Wang Yani—China's Extraordinary Young Artist.* Scholastic, 1991